Counselling for
Alcohol Problems

Counselling in Practice

Series editor: Windy Dryden
Associate editor: E. Thomas Dowd

Counselling in Practice is a series of books developed especially for counsellors and students of counselling, which provides practical, accessible guidelines for dealing with clients with specific, but very common, problems. Books in this series have become recognized as classic texts in their field, and include:

Counselling for Depression, second edition
Paul Gilbert

Counselling Survivors of Childhood Sexual Abuse, second edition
Claire Burke Draucker

Counselling for Post-Traumatic Stress Disorder, second edition
Michael J. Scott and Stephen G. Stradling

Counselling for Alcohol Problems, second edition
Richard Velleman

Counselling Couples
Donald L. Bubenzer and John D. West

Counselling People with Communication Problems
Peggy Dalton

Counselling for Anxiety Problems
Richard Hallam

Counselling for Grief and Bereavement
Geraldine M. Humphrey and David G. Zimpfer

Counselling for Stress Problems
Stephen Palmer and Windy Dryden

Counselling for Psychosomatic Problems
Diana Sanders

Counselling for Eating Disorders
Sara Gilbert

Counselling for
Alcohol Problems

Second Edition

Richard Velleman

 SAGE Publications

London ● Thousand Oaks ● New Delhi

SAGE Publications Ltd
1 Oliver's Yard, 55 City Road
London EC1Y 1SP

SAGE Publications Inc
2455 Teller Road
Thousand Oaks, California 91320

SAGE Publications India Pvt Ltd
B 1/I 1 Mohan Cooperative Industrial Area
Mathura Road,
New Delhi 110 044
India

SAGE Publications Asia-Pacific Pte Ltd
33 Pekin Street #02-01
Far East Square
Singapore 048763

British Library Cataloguing in Publication data

A catalogue record for this book is available
from the British Library

ISBN 978-0-7619-6578-7 (hbk)
ISBN 978-0-7619-6579-4 (pbk)

Library of Congress Control Number: 2001131039

Typeset by Mayhew Typesetting, Rhayader, Powys
Printed digitally and bound in Great Britain by
Biddles Ltd., King's Lynn, Norfolk

To my mother and father, sadly not alive to see this book; to Sophie and Bryonie, my lovely daughters; and to Gill, my partner, without whose encouragement the book would never have been finished!

Contents

Harry: a Case Example

Preface to the First Edition

What is this book about?

This book is about how to deal with alcohol problems. It is useful and practical, and contains advice and suggestions which people who deal with alcohol-related problems can use on a day-to-day basis.

Why is it needed?

Many counsellors work with clients who have problems with their use of alcohol – either as the main problem, or as one of many.

Many counsellors prefer to avoid the alcohol-related issues. Some hope the alcohol will cease to be a problem once other problems are dealt with; others avoid the issue because they are uncertain about how best to deal with it.

This book addresses these difficult areas, providing clear guidance and outlining the practical steps counsellors can take to deal with alcohol-related problems.

It is timely for such a book to be written. There is no practical guide which currently deals with these issues. Furthermore the past twenty years have brought many fresh insights, and many changes of attitude towards drinking problems; hence there is a need for effective practice to be summarized.

This book will be of interest to a wide range of practitioners, including specialist alcohol workers, general counsellors, clinical psychologists, social workers and probation workers, and especially to the many volunteer counsellors who are responsible for much of the counselling which occurs in alcohol advisory services across the country. I hope also that it will be of interest to members of the general public.

What is its orientation?

There is a huge range of approaches to understanding and dealing with alcohol problems. This implies that the alcohol field has not reached a stage of development where one clear set of ideas or one clear theory is accepted as the best or most useful way of understanding and dealing with these problems. People produce data, and speculation based upon this, concerning the influence of external factors such as culture, politics, economics, the media, and advertising; others study internal factors such as biology, genetics, personality, and socialization. There is little conclusive evidence, however, concerning the aetiological role or significance of any of these factors in alcohol-related problems, which may be created by a multiplicity of genetic, biochemical, psychological, social, and environmental factors. It therefore is one of the central arguments of this book that one should not attribute a single cause – or even the same patterns of causes – to alcohol problems. Instead, it is suggested that counsellors approach clients as individuals, attempting to understand, and hence enabling the client to understand, what he or she is doing, and why he or she is doing it.

Individual understanding does not mean the counsellor needs to engage in a deep, long-term relationship with the client, although in some cases it could; helping clients to reach this level of understanding can sometimes be achieved in only a few sessions. Nor does it mean clients cannot begin to deal with their problems until this understanding is reached: clients can begin to change their behaviour immediately counselling commences – and indeed, most will have started this change process before coming to see you; unless they start to understand themselves better, however, the change will not in most cases be maintained.

How is the book organized?

The book is divided into three sections. The first outlines the various approaches to alcohol-related problems, including causes and intervention.

The second section looks at the general area of intervention through counselling; the specific techniques that practitioners have developed and found useful over the years; the problem of relapse and how to understand and deal with it; and the issues of working in groups.

The third and final section examines a variety of difficult situations which may arise – or which counsellors often fear may arise – and looks at some of the particular problems which crop up for volunteer counsellors. It examines and explains some of the myths of working with problem drinkers; and it discusses working with the spouses and other family members of problem drinkers, both individually and as part of couple or family counselling.

Richard Velleman
September 1991

Preface to the Second Edition

Why a new book? What is new? What has changed?

In some ways, there is no need for a second edition of *Counselling for Alcohol Problems*. The basic thrust of the first edition was encapsulated in eight main points, and these have not changed. The eight points are that:

- people are individuals who do things for individual reasons;
- there are always reasons for people's behaviour;
- if people continue to use alcohol despite developing problems, this must also occur for reasons;
- alcohol use lies along a continuum: there is no simple dividing line between 'alcoholic' drinkers and the rest of the population;
- individuals can move along this continuum in either direction;
- individuals learn how to behave towards alcohol, and this is open to change;
- counselling draws out the client through a process of reflecting, clarifying, challenging, exploring;
- these activities are done with, not to, the client.

Furthermore, the main theoretically driven intervention ideas discussed in the first edition – the cycle of change, motivational interviewing, relapse management, controlled drinking, and so on – have not been overtaken by other, newer or more effective ways of intervening.

On the other hand, because this book has been utilized as a main core text for many of the courses in the UK which train counsellors to deal with alcohol problems, it is vital that the book is as up to date as possible. In the decade since the first edition, new evidence has emerged about the efficacy of some of the interventions discussed here (and particularly, Project MATCH [a major US research study on interventions with alcohol problems described in Chapter 2] has reported, with key evidence on how effective some of the ideas such as motivational or cognitive-behavioural approaches are, which are supported in this book); new medications have been developed to help deal with withdrawal syptoms; new methods of identification have been tried out; and new controversies have emerged. Furthermore, Project MATCH has also suggested that encouraging people to use Alcoholics Anonymous, whose approach I did not favour in the first edition, may also be very effective. Finally, the issue of dealing with people with both alcohol problems and mental health difficulties and/or illicit drug problems, has become far more widespread. This second edition has attempted to incorporate the most important of all of these new findings. And of course, many of the addresses and telephone numbers in the 'useful addresses' section at the end have changed and e-mail and web-site addresses (much more useful and well used than they might have been in the early 1990s) have been added where they are available.

The main changes, therefore, to this book are:

In **Part 1**

- drinking guidelines have been updated in line with current government recommendations, some of the prevalence and other factual information has been updated, and some of the ideas around causation have been revised (Chapter 1);
- considerably more has been added on medical help (including further information on new therapeutic drugs and on withdrawal symptoms), and further information is included on evidence-based approaches, especially the results of Project MATCH (Chapter 2).

In **Part 2**

- the 'cycle of change' ideas have been updated in line with latest thinking, and the newer ideas of the role of readiness, importance and confidence in the change process have been introduced (Chapter 3);
- further information has been added on assessing clients' stage of change, on new therapeutic drugs, on withdrawal symptoms, on assessing the physical effects of alcohol consumption, and on the evidence base underpinning various intervention methods, as has a brief discussion on the notions of craving and addiction (Chapter 4);
- dealing with lapse situations is further discussed, and ideas about 'programmed lapses' are further clarified (Chapter 5);

- problems arising in group settings (such as literacy, or clients' drinking) are briefly discussed (Chapter 6).

In **Part 3**

- common problems and difficulties are further discussed, including how best to deal with the disclosure of traumatic events, and working with (and dealing with confidentiality across) other agencies (Chapter 7);
- a brief chapter has been added on 'co-morbidity' – working with people who have both alcohol problems and another major problem (Chapter 8);
- the evidence is discussed that some drinking is good for you (Chapter 9);
- the latest evidence is discussed on how some forms of coping by family members with the drinking of their relatives is more effective than others (Chapter 10).

And in the **Appendices**

- information on facilities and how some of them work has been updated, as has the information in the 'Useful addresses' section.

Where appropriate, the references have been updated throughout.

Finally, I would like to comment on the status of the ideas in this book. I make many suggestions throughout the book, and clearly I believe that my suggestions are sensible. But it is important to emphasize the fact that these are just suggestions. As I say in the preface to the first edition, there is a huge range of approaches in this field, and we have not reached the stage where there is one dominant paradigm within the alcohol interventions area. The ideas and techniques described here should be seen as a tool kit from which people can select techniques as they seem appropriate. Counsellors must not undertake things that they are not comfortable with or do anything that countermands the policies under which the agency with which they work operates. All the ideas in this book will be useful for some counsellors; few will feel completely appropriate for everyone. It is important to recognize the difference between suggestions and prescriptions; and these are suggestions, not prescriptions

Richard Velleman
September 2000

Acknowledgements for the Second Edition

My grateful thanks go to the variety of individuals who responded to my request for suggestions as to how this book could be changed. Especial thanks go to Chris Johnstone for his host of extremely useful and helpful suggestions, to Anne Lingford-Hughes for her useful and clear updates on some of the newer drugs and other medical material, and also to Colin Bradbury, Ian Dickinson, Derek Fearnside, and Michael Hutchinson for their ideas. As with the commentaries on the manuscript of the first edition, I learnt a great deal from these suggestions, and incorporated many of them. I know that the book is considerably improved because of these; and the remaining faults are all my own!

Acknowledgements for the First Edition

My grateful thanks go to Gill Velleman and Sara-Jane Aris, who read and commented on the manuscript. I am especially grateful to Ken James, who provided a mass of highly detailed suggestions aimed at improving my style and phrasing. I learnt a great deal from them all, and incorporated very many of their suggestions and ideas.

I also want to acknowledge my debt to Thelma Fisher, for clarifying many of my ideas during our joint teaching of social work students during her time at the University of Bath. I have shamelessly borrowed from her handouts.

Finally, I want to thank Pip Mason for producing *Managing Drink*. The pack is full of good ideas, and thoughts as to how to present them; I have used many of them.

PART 1

APPROACHES

1

Understanding Alcohol Problems

Harry telephoned me, drunk and in tears. He had come to the end of his tether, and someone had advised him to phone me – I was his last resort. His wife, whom he loved very much, had died a year ago, and he had been drinking heavily ever since. He had tried Alcoholics Anonymous (AA), and a spell in an expensive private treatment centre, from which he had discharged himself after three days. Nothing had worked. Would I help?

Sue was worried that her third marriage might be on the rocks due to her drinking. Both she and her husband were heavy drinkers, but 'he can hold it', whereas Sue was increasingly acting in ways which embarrassed her husband and others. She realized that unless she did something she might lose her marriage, but she did not know what to do, given the lifestyle which she, her husband, and their whole circle of friends had adopted. What could I do?

Dick appeared at the alcohol advisory centre one day, angry and shouting. He had been referred everywhere, it seemed to him, and no one was prepared to help because he had a drinking problem. Everyone seemed to think he could not be trusted, that he was lying to them, and that he did not really want to be helped; he knew he did want help, but did not know what to do.

Marilyn, a single parent with two young children, was lonely and isolated. Her family, her ex-partner and his family all lived at the other end of the country; social services had her children on the at-risk register, and she did not know how to cope. The drinking, she said, was her way of turning an unbearable situation into one she could live with.

Martin took early retirement, possibly due to his drinking, and at the same time his father, whom he had planned on looking after, died very suddenly. Martin was married, with three school-age children, and his wife worked full-time. He felt depressed, although he did not think his drinking had any relationship to any of his problems.

This chapter deals with two main questions: 'what difficulties do these and other clients with alcohol-related problems pose for us as counsellors?' and 'how can we understand them?' The first question will be examined quite briefly, with the rest of the chapter being concerned with terminology and with the range of theories about the causes of alcohol problems.

What difficulties do clients with alcohol-related problems pose?

Working with clients with alcohol-related problems poses exactly the same set of difficulties as working with any other client group. There are problems which all clients share, irrespective of the area with which any agency is concerned or the issues any client initially presents.

However, in common with any other client group, there are difficulties which relate to the specific presenting problem, which could be bereavement, debt, marital crisis, and so on, but which in the case of this book is alcohol.

Let us look at these two issues in a bit more detail.

Similarities between all types of counselling

Wherever we work, the types of emotional difficulties with which clients present are similar. Whether or not we work in an agency specializing in alcohol, drugs, relationships, bereavement, sexual orientation; whether we work in social services, hospitals, community teams, education; whether we work in the statutory or the voluntary sector – there are common problems for people living in today's society.

Clients may present with any combination from a wide range of emotional, cognitive, behavioural, and practical difficulties. They may be overcome with grief (as Harry was), anger (as Dick was), uncertainty (as Sue was), bewilderment, depression, anxiety, and so on. They may have problems with their social lives, their relationships, the law, their jobs, their health, their finances, or housing.

People who have developed a problem with alcohol are still people – seeing a client with an alcohol problem does not mean that you as a counsellor will be faced with an entirely different set of issues than if you worked with any other sort of presenting problem.

The second similarity is that the counselling process is the same irrespective of the type of problem the client presents with. There are certain roles, functions, tasks, and responsibilities that we as counsellors have to fulfil, which do not differ depending on the sort of difficulty a client brings (Chapter 3).

Specific difficulties with alcohol problems
There are, however, particular difficulties which relate specifically to clients' alcohol consumption. These are usually concerned with two issues: that alcohol is an addictive drug which can give rise to problems of tolerance and withdrawal, dependency, craving, and a strong ambivalence about whether or not giving up or reducing use is either possible or desirable (see Chapter 4); and that public and professional attitudes to drinking problems are so negative that clients will often find it difficult to get help when they need it.

How can we understand alcohol-related difficulties?

This question relates to the issue of cause, and there are many theories which seek to explain the cause of alcohol problems. In particular this field has been bedevilled for decades by the simple misconception that there is a single cause of alcohol problems. This immediately raises two further questions: 'what do I mean by an alcohol problem?' and 'why am I so disparaging about there being a single cause?'

What is an 'alcohol problem' – the issue of terminology
My own definition of an alcohol problem is very simple: if someone's drinking causes problems for him or her, or for someone else, in any area of their lives, then that drinking is problematic. If someone's drinking causes problems with his or her health, finances, the law, work, friends, or relationships, then that drinking is problematic; if it causes problems for husbands, wives, children, parents, bosses, or subordinates, then that drinking is problematic.

There are many implications of such a simple definition. It means that whether or not someone has a drinking problem is not determined by fixed quantities of alcohol, or fixed timings, but instead is a matter of negotiation by the individual with him or herself, family, friends, workplace, and society as a whole.

The idea of negotiation within context may be illustrated by a few examples:

- Within a marital context, it might be that a person drinks one pint of beer a week but is married to a confirmed teetotaller: one pint may cause problems, and will need to be negotiated within the marital context.
- Within an employment context, someone might drink half a bottle of wine during a business lunch, or might visit the pub at lunchtime with colleagues. In some contexts, such drinking has been negotiated as acceptable behaviour; yet the same drinking may cause severe problems within an industry which has introduced an alcohol-at-work policy which forbids drinking during the working day.
- Within the social context, forty years ago someone's ability to drive after drinking was determined by their ability to walk a straight line; now this has been renegotiated by society such that it is determined by their blood-alcohol level, and if it exceeds a certain amount (and they are detected by the police!) they are automatically deemed unfit to drive, and will have their licence revoked.

Someone has an alcohol problem if their drinking causes them or anyone else a problem. This idea is gradually gaining acceptance, but there are still many phrases that are in common use, such as 'alcoholism', 'alcohol-dependence syndrome' (ADS), 'alcohol-related problems', 'social drinking', 'normal drinking', 'controlled drinking', and so on.

Problematic drinking

Various ways of understanding alcohol problems have been put forward. These include the following.

As a moral issue, with people who abuse alcohol being seen as morally degenerate. They are lacking in self-control, and should become social outcasts. This view is held by many people.

As a disease issue, where the abuse of alcohol is seen as the corollary of the chronic illness of alcoholism. Alcoholics are ill, and hence need care and concern, not moral outrage. Another form of this states that alcoholism is an allergic reaction to alcohol. This view is held by Alcoholics Anonymous, and by many health and other care practitioners.

Although this disease view has been with us for a long time (Orford, 1985), it was helped along by the formation of AA in the 1930s, and especially by the publication of a book entitled *The Disease Concept of Alcoholism* (Jellinek, 1960), in which the author suggested there were five types of alcoholism:

- alpha – psychological dependence on alcohol, no physical dependence;
- beta – heavy drinking resulting in physical damage, but no dependence;
- gamma – physical dependence with loss of control when drinking;
- delta – inability to abstain for even short periods;
- epsilon – long periods of abstinence plus bouts or binges.

There are, of course, huge problems inherent in these distinctions. Can one distinguish between psychological and physical dependence? Or between loss of control and inability to abstain? Nevertheless, the categories underline an already apparent point: there exists great variety in the way an individual can misuse alcohol.

There are both advantages and disadvantages to using the term 'alcoholism'. Many people find the disease concept useful, and conceptualizing it as an illness has allowed a far more valuable approach to be developed within the workplace, where people with alcohol-related problems can be helped to overcome their difficulties as opposed to being sent immediately down the disciplinary route. Disadvantages include the fact that 'alcoholism' is often used as a generic label, implying a single entity; this in turn has led to expensive and fruitless searches for both a single cause and an all-embracing cure. Furthermore the idea of the 'disease' of alcoholism suggests a medical problem, where people are seen as physically addicted and are subject to powerful cravings for alcohol. This medicalization links it with a whole range of beliefs concerning diseases and illnesses held in our society: treatment is the job of the medical profession; there is nothing I can do about my drinking – the solution is not my responsibility, it is the doctor's; and so on. The term also dissuades many people from seeking help either because they do not want to be labelled an 'alcoholic', or because they are sure their drinking, even though it may be causing some 'slight' problems, is nothing like the stereotype of what an alcoholic is like.

Because of some of these reasons, the World Health Organization (WHO) in 1977 suggested replacing the term 'alcoholism' with 'alcohol-dependence syndrome' (ADS). In many ways, this is an improvement. It suggests that a drinking problem can be described in terms of three factors: the degree to which a person's drinking behaviour is abnormal; they feel there is something wrong with their drinking; or they have an altered physiological response to alcohol (tolerance/withdrawal symptoms).

Hence the definition accepts that there are three indices which need to be measured – behavioural, subjective, and physiological; these are all continua running from normal to highly abnormal, and it is possible for a person to be high on one or two dimensions without necessarily being high on all. However, although ADS has replaced 'alcoholism', it is the latter term which is commonly used by both the general and the counselling public.

Many people argue that, although the development of the ADS is an improvement, it is still a medical disease notion of what is fundamentally a non-medical problem; although others argue that because people do develop problems with their consumption of an addictive drug, it is reasonable to use such a medical notion.

It is clear that there are both positives and negatives associated with the notions of alcoholism and alcohol dependence syndrome.

A final way of viewing problem drinking is as an issue relating to the problems caused by alcohol, for example, problems with health, the law, work, family, social life, violence, and so on. This is the position taken by this book, as outlined earlier.

Having discussed what problematic drinking might mean, some of the other terms need explanation.

Social drinking

This is often juxtaposed with problem drinking, as in 'I don't have a problem with my drinking; it is purely social.' However, a person's drinking can be *both* problematic, in that it has caused or is causing them problems with, for example, their health or finances *and* social, in that they drink in company or in social situations, and they do not drink more than their peers. So 'social' relates to the context in which someone drinks – with friends, as opposed to solitary drinking – and not to whether or not this drinking leads to problems.

Normal drinking

This term is used in a variety of ways. Often it is used synonymously with social drinking, and suffers from the same confusions. At other times, 'normal' is used to imply that a comparison is being made between the drinking of the person in question, and the drinking of a wide range of other people. Within this latter group, some people will be drinking a great deal more than others, some will be drinking a great deal less, and many will be near some middle point in terms of the quantity consumed, the frequency, and so on. So sometimes 'normal' is used to describe drinking which is no different to the majority of other drinkers.

The difficulty here is, with whom is the person comparing him or herself? When people talk about 'normal' drinking they are usually referring to drinking which does not seem excessive in relation to their perceptions of what other people drink, and they might be wrong. Even if an individual is correct in his or her estimate of how much other people drink, this does not mean that these other people are drinking in a problem-free way – they may also be drinking at a level that could lead to problems.

There are many people who are drinking at an excessive level, and are causing themselves and others immense problems. A quick examination of the huge range of available statistics reveals that:

- 35 per cent of male and 21 per cent of female single persons drink in excess of sensible limits – corresponding figures for married men and women are 24 per cent and 13 per cent;
- between 5 and 10 per cent of both boys and girls aged 14–15 are drinking more than the recommended levels for adults; under-age consumption of alcohol is often a precursor to smoking and the use of illicit drugs, and the risk of smoking and drug use is particularly high in adolescents who report high levels of drunkenness;
- over two million people in England and Wales, and up to 15 million people in the US, have alcohol-related problems; on a typical day in the UK, some 10,000 individuals seek help for their own or someone else's drinking problem;
- around 25 per cent of British men and 8 per cent of British women, or 17 per cent of the total post-war generation, run the risk of developing an alcohol problem at some stage in their lives;
- each of these individuals will have contact with and will influence a wide range of others: family members, friends, workmates, members of the public (who share the same roads as intoxicated drinkers);
- the number of people who may need information, advice, and counselling related to their own or someone else's alcohol problems is huge, representing people at all points on a continuum, from relatively early and mild difficulties at one end, to serious and life-threatening concerns at the other.

The seriousness of some of these issues cannot be overstated:

- Deaths attributable to alcohol consumption are estimated to lie in the region of 40,000 per year in England and Wales, and

100,000 per year in the US. (By comparison deaths from illicit drug use in England and Wales are estimated to be fewer than 1,500 per year.)

- Within these figures of alcohol-related deaths, 66 per cent of deaths by fire, and between 33 and 66 per cent (depending on the time of day) of deaths on the road are alcohol-related.
- About 50 per cent of all crime is alcohol-related; as is around 80 per cent of domestic violence, and 30 per cent of divorces. Between 12 and 27 per cent of men admitted to general medical wards in general (not psychiatric) hospitals have alcohol-related problems; and at least 20 per cent of child abuse cases are alcohol-related.

'Normal' drinking, then, may certainly not be harmless drinking! But if that is the case, people need to know how much alcohol they can safely consume before their drinking puts them at risk. There are a number of useful guides in the UK which answer this question and some are listed at the end of this chapter. Briefly, alcohol is usefully measured in 'units' in the UK and in 'drinks' in the US, with one unit (or one drink) of alcohol in each of the following: half a pint of ordinary-strength beer or lager (12 oz bottle of beer in the US), one glass of wine, one pub single measure of spirits (1 oz in the US), or one pub measure of sherry/martini (2.5 oz in the US). A quick formula for working out the number of units in larger quantities of a drink is to multiply the volume of the drink in millilitres (ml) by the alcohol content and then divide by 1,000. Therefore a bottle of wine (750 ml) with an alcohol content of 12 per cent = 750 (size of bottle) × 12 (alcohol content) ÷ 1,000 = 9. The bottle of wine contains 9 units.

Guidelines for sensible drinking have been agreed in the UK between all the relevant authorities. The advice used to be that if women drink less than 14 units of alcohol, or men drink less than 21 units, spread throughout the week in both cases, then there is almost no risk to their health. If women drink between 14 and 21 units, or men between 21 and 35 units, they are within the at-risk zone; once a woman drinks above 21 units, or a man drinks above 35 units, they are drinking dangerously.

It is now considered more helpful to view this guidance in daily terms (otherwise people feel that they can drink their weekly limit in just one day, or over the weekend) and it is therefore recommended that men should drink no more than 3 to 4 units a day and women no more than 2 to 3 units a day; and that it is a good idea to have one or two alcohol-free days in each week.

Men consistently drinking 4 units a day and women consistently drinking 3 units a day incur a progressive health risk.

These, however, are general guidelines, and they relate primarily to health. Other problems can occur at much lower levels of drinking; and people who are pregnant, on medication, who are very young or inexperienced drinkers, or elderly, may well have far lower limits. There is also some evidence relating to the health benefits that can accrue from very light drinking: this issue is summarized in Chapter 9.

Controlled drinking

This term has a very precise meaning, and is examined in greater detail in Chapter 4. Briefly, it means that people who control their drinking examine carefully how much they drink, and keep precisely to determined limits. 'Limited drinking' is sometimes used synonymously.

A single cause?

I have three reasons why I believe alcohol problems should not be attributed to a single cause. First, even if it were the case that all alcohol problems present themselves in exactly the same way, there is no need to think they all stem from the same cause. This is similar to saying that because visitors are in London, they must have travelled there by the same method.

The second reason is that it is certainly not the case that all alcohol problems present in the same way. Many people think they do, and this is an area where stereotypes abound. The common perception of someone with alcohol problems is of a scruffy, destitute person, usually male, on a park bench, with a bottle. The reality is that the range of people with alcohol-related problems is vast. This diversity is apparent in every area, be it the client group, the type of alcoholic beverage used, or the nature of the problem generated by the alcohol misuse. It makes much more sense to suggest that there are many reasons why people develop problems with their alcohol use, and that part of the job of a counsellor is to help the client to discover which reasons apply to him or her.

The final reason is that there is no evidence that only one cause exists. In fact, many of the proposed causes have no evidence at all to back them up, and most have only a bit of evidence, which implies that many of these causes may be the cause for some people some of the time, but none of them are the single cause which so many people have been searching for.

The message in this book is that, even if one believes that 'alcoholism' is a useful term, this is not the most helpful place for either clients or counsellors to start. Hence instead of asking the question of oneself or of the client, 'Is this man or woman an alcoholic?' or even 'Do they have the alcohol-dependence syndrome?', a more helpful question is: *'What factors made this man or woman drink so much or so inappropriately?'* and, *'What can I do to help him or her to deal with these particular factors in the future?'*

So what does cause alcohol problems?

The range of explanations and theories put forward to identify why some people develop problems with their alcohol use is astounding. Although there is some evidence to support some (although by no means all) of these theories, there is no evidence that any one of them provides all, or even most, of the answers. We need to know what some of these theories are for a number of reasons: it is important to know what some people – including many of our clients – believe about the causes of alcohol problems; as counsellors we must equip ourselves with a number of different theories which we can use in thinking about particular clients; and finally, the very existence of so many theories underlines how vital it is to keep an open mind when seeing clients.

Factors within the individual

The ideas examined here relate to the belief that the reason why some people develop problems with their drinking has something to do with them as individuals.

The idea that the problem drinker has 'got something' which 'normals' do not have has been around for a long time, although there is little evidence in its favour. There are three common forms of this idea, each suggesting that problem drinkers, or alcoholics, have got a slightly different 'thing'.

PSYCHIATRIC ILLNESS   This version of the idea suggests that people develop a psychiatric illness or disease named 'alcoholism' (or the alcohol-dependence syndrome). Over the past twenty years this view has increasingly been attacked, as evidence mounts that all the fundamental tenets are incorrect (Heather and Robertson, 1997: Chapters 3–5).

ALCOHOLIC PERSONALITY   More research money and time have been spent on this area than almost any other in the alcohol field. Literally thousands of studies have been published attempting to document the 'alcoholic personality'. There are two different ideas at work here. The first is that if someone drinks a great deal over a period of many years, his or her personality changes. There is a lot of evidence to support this theory. The second idea is that there is a type of personality which predisposes some people, or even causes them, to develop a problem. In this case, although people have searched a huge range of areas, no useful and consistent results on the 'pre-alcoholic' personality have been forthcoming.

ALLERGY   This simply suggests that some people have an allergic reaction to alcohol. This theory posits that 'alcoholics' are 'normal' people until they drink alcohol; once they do, they suffer an allergic reaction, which sets up a craving to drink more and more. This theory is at the heart of the disease model of alcoholism. However, there is not one shred of evidence to back it up.

Another set of ideas is that the problem drinker lacks something 'normals' have got. Given the failure to demonstrate that people with alcohol problems are different from 'normal' people by virtue of having something, the suggestion here is that what is wrong with them is that they do *not* have 'something' which 'normal' people have.

The first proposition is the idea that 'normal' people do not develop problems because the consequences of drinking a lot – feeling sick and dizzy, being sick, and having a hangover – all stop them from developing a problem. Perhaps people who develop a drinking problem simply do not get hangovers, and so on, and thus continue drinking until they develop a serious problem. When interviewed, many problem drinkers said this was true for them; other problem drinkers, however, said they felt and were sick, had awful hangovers, and yet still developed problems.

The next idea is that maybe problem drinkers are lacking a mechanism to monitor their internal blood-alcohol level. The presumption here is that most people can and do monitor their blood-alcohol level by focusing on such internal cues as feeling tipsy or dizzy, and they stop drinking when their internal monitoring suggests they have had enough. Perhaps problem drinkers lack this system, and hence do not know when to stop? However, it was discovered that people without drinking problems also lacked such a system. While everyone (including problem drinkers) recognizes some internal cues, they do not do it by monitoring blood-alcohol levels. One's perception of one's level of intoxication varies hugely with mood – a person can feel anywhere between very intoxicated to not at all so, with the same blood-alcohol level; furthermore most people seem to regulate their drinking via external cues, such as recalling how many drinks they have had, as well as via monitoring their level of tipsiness.

Given the failure of these attempts to show that problem drinkers are different in some way, it was only a matter of time before some people realized that people who behaved in ways which led to alcohol problems must be doing so for reasons. There are two reasons suggested. First, that drinking makes the drinker feel better by heightening current positive feelings; providing escape from negative feelings (depression, boredom, low self-esteem, tension, and anxiety); and providing relief from withdrawal symptoms. And second, that it allows him or her to do things which would not normally be allowed (aggression, attention-seeking, expressing sexuality).

All the ideas so far presented suffer from the fact that they are seeking one cause to explain all problem drinking; and they are all based on individual issues. Yet drinking occurs within a wide social context; and there are theories relating to that as well.

Factors within the social context

The ideas in this section relate to the belief that for people who develop problems with their drinking it is not a matter of having individual reasons for drinking excessively, but of learning, or being pressured by others, to drink too much.

It has been recognized for many years that drinking problems run in families; between 30 and 40 per cent of problem drinkers report having one or both parents who was also a problem drinker. Why should problems be transmitted from one generation to another?

MODELLING FROM PARENTS   Parental behaviour is the biggest single influence on the long-term behaviour of children. Parental attitudes and behaviour create expectations and values about drinking; and depending on the degree of identification with the parental drinker, the child is more likely to follow in their footsteps. Even if the growing child vows never to put their family through the same set of experiences, once adult pressures mount the child may have to turn to the only coping mechanism which he or she has seen modelled by a parent – excessive drinking. Nevertheless, problem drinking cannot be blamed solely on problem drinking parents – most problem drinkers do not have such parents, and many children of such parents do not in turn develop drinking problems.

GENETIC VULNERABILITY   Although research in this area is difficult, it is clear there is some genetic influence in problem drinking. This genetic link, however, only seems to apply to a small percentage of problem drinkers; it is still uncertain what it is that may be transmitted genetically, but what the genetic linkage shows is that certain individuals may be more vulnerable to developing an alcohol problem, not that they certainly will develop one. The research implies an increased risk, which leads to an increased probability of developing a problem; it does not imply predetermination.

UNSTABLE HOME ENVIRONMENT   Many people have argued that the most likely cause of problem drinking is the effects of instability – that is, the growing child experiencing conflict between or with parents, parental absences, or early parental loss following marital breakup.

There is increasing evidence that these factors are important in determining whether or not problems are transmitted from one generation to another.

One's peer group, especially during adolescence, and even in adulthood, is highly important as well.

People often model themselves on their peers, and this will often involve the development of both attitudes and behaviour which mimic the model. Alcohol has a range of socially ascribed meanings attached to it – for both young men and young women, of being older, of being sexual; and for young men of being masculine and being violent – all of which might link with a young person's desire to be accepted. Some of this modelling can occur as a result of pressure from peers. Sometimes this pressure is overt, sometimes covert; and it does not stop once adolescence is over. Researchers have shown that, within a group, the speed with which people drink is influenced by the speed of the fastest drinker: the more he or she drinks, the more others feel pressured to drink more.

The influence of others is not confined to a group of close friends. For example, some professions have more problem drinkers than others. A number of factors influence this, including: availability – if you work with alcohol (selling it, making it, and so on); lack of supervision – if you are unmonitored or work alone; if your job involves entertaining (public relations, selling, and so on); if your normal family and sexual relationships are disrupted (in the armed forces, working abroad, travelling salesman, and so on); or if alcohol is made available to you cheaply as part of your working conditions. In all of these circumstances you are more likely to drink more.

National and cultural conditions

All the ways of understanding problem drinking so far have been based on thinking about people who develop problems with their alcohol use. However, the ideas in this section suggest that the reasons why people develop alcohol problems are connected to society as a whole.

One view suggests it is society and social problems which cause people to turn to alcohol or drugs: society is unfair – in a just society where people are equal and have control over their lives, there would be no alcohol problems. Hence it is argued that people drink excessively because of their social conditions; they seek to escape from unemployment, and from environmental deprivation such as inadequate housing and poverty.

Another view suggests that problems arise due to the way society deals with alcohol because individuals are not taught to use alcohol in a sensible way in Britain and America. Instead of alcohol being introduced 'normally' to young people as they grow up, it is restricted to licensed premises, and to 'adults'. It is argued that it is not surprising that many young people feel that drinking alcohol is a major route to becoming 'adult'.

A final view suggests that the problem is simply the existence and availability of addictive substances such as alcohol. This view states that we are all at risk of developing alcohol-related problems simply by being exposed (and cajoled by advertisers into drinking more). Indeed, there exists considerable evidence supporting this view, in that the number and range of alcohol-related problems within a country appear to be directly proportional to the amount of alcohol consumed by that country. Holders of this view argue for reducing the high profile of alcohol within our society, and increasing the range of accessible alternatives to drinking.

Availability is currently seen as significant in understanding why alcohol problems are rising across the Western world, with factors influencing availability including: quantity, cost, accessibility, knowledge that alcoholic drinks are available, of the effects of alcohol, and that alcohol is considered by society in certain ways.

All these national and cultural theories are linked. The European style of drinking, especially in France, is often cited as an example of how alcohol need not be made into such a major issue. France does have lower levels of alcohol-related violence, and fewer alcohol-related city-centre disturbances; however, it has far higher levels of other alcohol-related harm, such as liver disease, other medical problems and drink driving accidents.

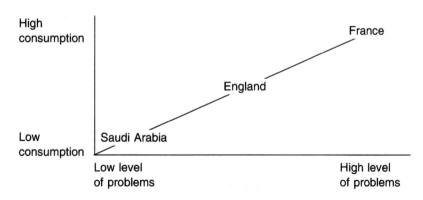

Figure 1.1   *Alcohol consumption per country*

The various problems relate to the overall style of drinking within different countries. For example, many European countries have developed a particular style of using alcohol – high avail-ability, few restrictions, drinking being acceptable throughout the day – which has led to very high average levels of alcohol consumption.

Such a drinking pattern, however, does not lead to the sudden intoxication which seems so strongly linked to violence and social disturbances. Instead, it leads to a habitually high blood-alcohol level, which results in a far higher incidence of medical problems. The UK system of restricting the public consumption of alcohol and keeping prices relatively high leads to an overall lower level of average consumption with fewer medical problems, but to more frequent occasions of sudden intoxication.

The more alcohol, on average, is consumed by people within a country, the more problems with alcohol that country has (Figure 1.1). The way alcohol is consumed largely determines the sort of problems the country will experience: restricted use over short periods will lead to greater problems with sudden intoxication; unrestricted access will lead to greater health problems.

'Two-factor' and 'three-factor' theories

The preceding pages have examined many theories relating to individual, social, and cultural causes of alcohol problems. It is my view that all or most of these ideas can be useful sometimes. How, though, can they be linked together?

There has been a development in other areas (such as the study of depression and schizophrenia) of so-called 'two-factor' theories, which simply means there are two sets of factors at work: vulnerability factors, and triggering, or precipitating, factors. These ideas suggest that everyone is vulnerable to or at risk of developing some problem or other. For some people, their risk is of depression, for others anxiety, for yet others some physical problem such as cancer or coronary problems; and for some, alcohol problems.

Vulnerability to developing any of these problems will exist on a continuum from 'highly vulnerable' to 'very invulnerable'. Why some people are more at risk than others in relation to one problem rather than another is insufficiently understood at present, but probable factors relating to vulnerability include: genetic, personality, patterns of upbringing and experience, physiological factors, and (as far as alcohol problems are concerned) alcohol consumption patterns.

The two-factor idea suggests that although everyone is vulnerable to one sort of problem or another – or maybe to more than one problem – even those who are vulnerable will need some triggering factor(s) to push them towards developing a problem. The theory also suggests that a range of factors could trigger or precipitate someone into developing a problem. Probable triggering factors include: stress, other psychological factors, social factors, and availability.

These two-factor ideas are useful in the alcohol field as well, with the addition of a third factor. Chris Johnstone, a colleague in Bristol, uses the term 'the three Ps', suggesting that there are 'predisposing', 'precipitating', and 'perpetuating' factors, with predisposing factors including the 'vulnerability' ones listed above; precipitating factors again being those listed above; but with the addition of perpetuating factors, which are those which maintain or perpetuate heavy drinking once it has started, and even once people have developed serious problems. This is important: most people who develop drinking problems change their behaviour without recourse to outside help. This implies that the ones who need our assistance will have perpetuating factors in their lives which block them from changing.

These two- and three-factor ideas suggest, then, that there will be some people who are more at risk of developing an alcohol problem, either because they have greater vulnerability to alcohol problems, or because they have more triggers to develop such a problem; and the theory suggests that everyone could develop an alcohol problem if the triggers were sufficiently strong. Because of availability and/or pressures to drink – either on the job or from their peer group – and/or personal problems, the following are among those who are more at risk of developing an alcohol problem:

- generally tense or socially anxious individuals;
- children of problem drinkers/drug-takers;
- children of publicans/off-licence owners;
- those who work in certain occupations (the production, distribution and selling of alcohol or drugs; in the hotel and catering trades; as seamen; in the armed services; as commercial travellers; in entertainment; as customs officials or as medical practitioners).

Conclusion

It is probable that all the ideas I have outlined in this chapter are true for some people at some time, but none of the ideas are the only cause of all alcohol problems.

Harry, Sue, Dick, Marilyn, and Martin all have different problems with alcohol, all caused by different reasons, and all amenable to being helped in different ways. This means that, even if one believes that 'alcoholism' is a useful term, being able to answer the question 'Is this man or woman an alcoholic?' or even, 'Do they have alcohol-dependence syndrome?' will not provide many helpful ways of developing one's counselling relationship. When counselling someone with an alcohol-related problem, a more useful starting point should be: *'What factors made this man or woman drink so much, and therefore what can I do to help him or her to deal with these particular factors in the future?'*

Key points

- Clients with problems with their drinking come to us in a wide variety of ways, bearing a wide variety of difficulties.
- Clients with alcohol problems are individuals living within our society, and are prey to the same stresses and strains as we all are. The difficulties they present, then, will be similar to those which clients with any other sort of problem show.
- We will help them by using the same skills, and the same understanding of the counselling process, that we use with any other kind of presenting problem.
- There will be specific issues relating to alcohol which we ought to understand. This will increase our self-confidence in working with the clients.
- There are many issues of terminology within the alcohol field, with different terms revealing important values counsellors and others hold about the ways in which clients change.

- For me, if someone's drinking is causing problems in any area of his or her life, then that drinking is problematic.
- I come out firmly against the idea of a single cause for alcohol problems. People must be dealt with on an individual basis, not according to some pre-existing formula based on any single theory of causation.
- There are a large number of theories examining the causes of alcohol problems. Some are based on factors within the individual, some on factors within the social context, and others on overall cultural factors.
- I suggest that vulnerability towards developing a problem with alcohol exists on a continuum, from highly vulnerable to very invulnerable. Even highly invulnerable individuals could develop a problem with their use of alcohol, given the right circumstances. I also suggest that even those people who are most vulnerable will need some triggering factor(s) to push them towards developing a problem.
- Finally, most people who develop problems change without recourse to outside help. This implies that the ones who need our assistance will have perpetuating factors in their lives which block them from changing.

References and further reading

General
Faculty of Public Health Medicine (1991) *Alcohol and the Public Health*. London: Macmillan.
Heather, N. and Robertson, I. (1997) *Problem Drinking* (2nd edn). Oxford: Oxford University Press.
Jellinek, E. (1960) *The Disease Concept of Alcoholism*. New Brunswick, NJ: Hillhouse.
Kent, R. (1996) *Talking it through: the National Alcohol Concern Vocational Training Pack*. London: Alcohol Concern.
Orford, J. (1985) *Excessive Appetites*. Chichester: Wiley.
Plant, M., Single, E. and Stockwell, T. (eds) (1997) *Alcohol: Minimising the Harm. What Works?* London: Free Association Books.
Velleman, R. (1997) 'Counselling people with alcohol and drug problems', in S. Palmer and G. McMahon (eds) *The Handbook of Counselling, Second Edition*. London: Routledge.

Information about alcohol
Alcohol Concern (2000) *Fact Sheet 4: One in Twenty-five Adults Dependent on Alcohol in UK*. London: Alcohol Concern.
Alcohol Concern (2000) *Fact Sheet 18: Alcohol and UK Mortality*. London: Alcohol Concern.

Alcohol Concern (2000) *Fact Sheet 20: Alcohol and UK Accidents*. London: Alcohol Concern.

Anonymous (1998) *The Big List: the Ultimate Guide to Alcohol Units*. London: Hard Rain Productions.

Faculty of Public Health Medicine (1991) *Alcohol and the Public Health*. London: Macmillan.

Hussein Rassool, G. (ed.) (1998) *Substance Use and Misuse: Nature, Context and Clinical Interventions*. Oxford: Blackwell Science.

Raistrick, D., Hodgson, R. and Ritson, B. (eds) (1999) *Tackling Alcohol Together. The Evidence Base for a UK Alcohol Policy*. London: Free Association Books.

Royal College of General Practitioners (1986) *Alcohol – a Balanced View*. London: Royal College of General Practitioners.

Royal College of Physicians (1987) *A Great and Growing Evil – the Medical Consequences of Alcohol Abuse*. London: Tavistock.

Royal College of Psychiatrists (1986) *Alcohol – Our Favourite Drug*. London: Tavistock.

Secretary of Health and Human Services (1987) *Sixth Special Report to the US Congress on Alcohol and Health*. Washington, DC: US Department of Health and Human Services.

2

Therapeutic Approaches

A s we have seen, there are many theories as to why people develop drinking problems. Each of these theories has generated its own methods and techniques for intervening with alcohol problems, and some of them are incompatible with one another. In this chapter, an outline is presented of the range of facilities and agencies which offer help to people with drinking problems. Some of the ways of helping which these facilities offer are then briefly described, before we go on to consider the general or usual package offered by many treatment or intervention agencies.

Facilities offering help

It is important to recognize that formal intervention is not the only way to deal with drinking problems. The fact is that the majority of people control or stop their drinking without any outside professional help at all. Some do this by monitoring their consumption and its effects; others respond to and are helped by comments about the nature and extent of their drinking from a spouse, a colleague or supervisor, a neighbour, or a friend; and yet others move in and out of drinking problems over their life span – due to, for example, altering lifestyles, varying levels of stress, and changing patterns of interaction with different social or work groups. For a substantial minority, however, some sort of formal help is useful. What facilities are there on offer for such individuals?

The range of possible agencies is large; the main types are briefly described at the end of this book. They can be usefully summarized as comprising five types of facilities provided by:

- people who volunteer their time;
- non-statutory agencies which are supported by grants, fund raising, and other external funding;

- statutory authorities, such as NHS Trusts or local authority social services;
- private organizations which charge for their services;
- employers, usually via welfare or personnel departments.

If as a counsellor working for one of these agencies you provide services to another organization (via 'outreach' or as part of a contract between your organization and another one) you must familiarize yourself with the other organization's aims and objectives, procedures, health & safety arrangements, and so on. You also need to be clear about their policies on confidentiality, and whether or not they match those held by your own agency.

What kind of help is offered?

All the agencies described above provide one or more forms of help from the range described below.

Medical help

This is usually in the form of medically prescribed drugs, which can usefully work as adjuncts to any other form of therapy, including counselling. In the main, there are two types of drug in use. Some drugs are used to control withdrawal symptoms which can occur when stopping using alcohol, and in particular to prevent fits and delirium tremens (DTs). Others are used to help people remain abstinent from alcohol. As well as these, people with alcohol problems are often also prescribed antidepressants, and anti-anxiety medication, as useful adjuncts to other forms of help.

The most common types of drug used to control withdrawal symptoms and prevent fits and DTs are the benzodiazepines such as Librium (chlordiazepoxide) or Valium (diazepam), and Heminevrin (chlormethiazole). The *benzodiazepines* (often termed 'minor tranquillizers') are particularly useful within community and out-patient settings. Their major drawback is that it is very easy to become dependent upon benzodiazepines, so many clients can simply switch dependencies. *Heminevrin* is also used to reduce severe withdrawal effects from alcohol. Its major drawback is that it is very easy for somone to fatally overdose if they take it while they are still drinking. For this reason, Heminevrin is no longer recommended for use outside an in-patient setting. A further drawback, as with the benzodiazepines, is that it is very easy to become dependent upon it. Increasingly, clients are also prescribed supplements of the B1 vitamin, thiamine, for around a month after starting withdrawal.

The most common types of drug used to help people remain abstinent from alcohol is Antabuse (disulfiram), although the newer drugs of acamprosate and naltrexone are also becoming more widely used. *Antabuse* is a drug that has no physical effect unless someone consumes alcohol, whereupon it has very unpleasant effects. Antabuse works not only because of these physical effects, but also because of the *expectation* of the negative effects if alcohol is drunk. Its major drawbacks are that a client can easily stop taking the drug when he or she 'decides' to have a relapse; and it can be counter-therapeutic in that it reinforces clients' beliefs that they cannot control themselves without external means. On the other hand, there are also many positives. Many reviews of treatment effectiveness have shown that success rates are higher if Antabuse is used alongside other interventions. Antabuse remains in the body for some time, and hence, even if someone does decide to stop taking it, they still cannot drink for a while. As one client said: 'When I want a drink I want it now, not in a week.' Antabuse gives people thinking time, limiting the risk of drinking on impulse. Finally, programmes of supervised consumption, where a client takes Antabuse on a daily basis under the supervision of a member of their primary care team, again reduce relapse rates, and also provide 'early warning' of an impending relapse. *Acamprosate* is a derivative of a natural amino acid called taurine. It has been shown to approximately double the rate of abstinence from alcohol. It is thought to interfere with the functioning of areas of the brain to do with the desire to drink alcohol and with 'craving'. As with other drugs, acamprosate is likely to work best if used in conjunction with other help and not in isolation. Unlike Antabuse, it is safe to drink alcohol if you are taking acamprosate, but there is evidence to suggest that if someone taking acamprosate does re-start drinking, any relapse might be less severe. Acamprosate is also safe to use alongside Antabuse, and because the two drugs do very different things, using them in combination might offer a client a greater chance of remaining abstinent. *Naltrexone* is also a drug used to help people remain abstinent. It works by blocking activity of 'opiates' in the brain which are thought to be responsible for mediating pleasure or a 'high'. As with acamprosate, naltrexone has been shown both to increase the amount of time before drinking alcohol again, and to prevent a full-blown relapse if any alcohol is drunk. It is currently used more widely in the UK for helping people with opiate problems remain 'clean', although it is used widely in the US with alcohol problems.

Antidepressants are also sometimes prescribed. Some people with alcohol problems are prescribed antidepressants by their GP before it is realized that there is a serious alcohol problem. Others are given them in order to deal with the mood changes which sometimes follow stopping drinking. However, there is also a strong argument for not prescribing them. If people who have previously been drinking very heavily stop drinking, mood tends to improve anyway. Just stopping drinking can lead to such an improvement in mood, and reduction in anxiety, sleeping problems, etc., that I often encourage clients to hold on and ride out the difficulties and wait for this improvement, rather than moving in early with medication. If someone is still depressed a month after stopping drinking, or if there is serious risk of self-harm, then there is more of a case for prescribing.

Although the medications outlined above can be a very useful adjunct to other work with clients, it needs to be stressed that these are not wonder drugs. Every client has to understand that the key to overcoming alcohol problems is not taking medication (although that can be useful), but understanding why he or she is drinking, and what he or she can do to develop different ways of dealing with the world so that there is no need to drink in this harmful way in the future.

Individual help

This is usually in the form of counselling and various forms of psychotherapy. The basic idea is to talk through the problem of drinking and associated problems to try to help the person change. It is done in different agencies in different ways, some adopting a particular style of psychotherapy – for example, a cognitive-behavioural approach where the relationship between how people think about things and what they do is worked with – while others work eclectically. Chapters 3–5 cover issues concerning individual work in more detail.

Group help

This is usually offered either in the form of an Alcoholics Anonymous (AA) group, or one derived from it, or in a therapeutic group. AA groups offer self-help and support through the members sharing their own experiences with other 'alcoholics'. AA is strongly associated with the disease concept of 'alcoholism', and uses the 12-step approach.

AA methods revolve around a combination of group pressure, group cohesion, and caring. Many people find AA almost evangelical, and it has both the benefits and the drawbacks of that: it can turn people away, or it can lead to great commitment to the group and to the philosophy. AA believes that total abstinence is the only goal.

AA has helped many people throughout the world to stop drinking and although it has proved a difficult organization to evaluate, anything that works must be applauded. But its fundamental tenets – that alcoholism is an incurable disease, that people with alcohol problems have (and can have) no control over their drinking – are opposed to the beliefs expressed in this book.

There also are many types of non-AA therapeutic groups, including ones orientated towards providing social skills, insight into problems, coping with an alcohol-free lifestyle, confrontation, and education about alcohol (see Chapter 6).

Marital, relationship, and family work

Again there are many types, although most share the philosophy of seeing alcohol problems in the context of an individual's relationships (Chapter 9).

Which sort of help?

While there exists a range of facilities, and a range of services which these facilities might offer, no one agency offers the whole range of interventions. Why do some agencies, or some sorts of counsellors within agencies, offer one sort of help, whereas others offer a different kind?

One reason might be because some agencies offer help which is more evidence-based. That is, the agency only offers a form of help if there is good evidence to suggest that this way of working is more likely to help someone with an alcohol problem. Unfortunately, very few agencies explicitly review (on the basis of available evidence of effectiveness) the therapeutic approaches which they offer, which is a pity because it would now be possible to do this. There is clear evidence that some forms of help are better than others. Bill Miller in the USA has been at the forefront for many years of an approach which compares the outcomes of different types of help. This allows us to see which forms of help are more likely, and which are less likely, to work (see for example, Miller et al., 1998). The work of Miller and his colleagues, and of others working in this same tradition, has shown that some interventions (such as brief intervenions, motivational approaches, or social skills training) are far more effective than are others (such as educational films or lectures, confrontational counselling, or relaxation training). These findings do have to be treated sensibly, of course. As Miller et al. state: 'this is not to say that all clients benefit from [e.g.] social skills training, or that no client ever benefits from educational lectures and films. It is a matter of relative probabilities' (p. 208).

What is also becoming evident is that, if one looks only at the methods of intervention for which there is the most evidence, it is not clear that any one of these 'good' methods of helping people is better than any other. Although this statement can be supported in many ways, the most telling support comes from Project MATCH, the largest, most statistically powerful and most methodologically rigorous psychotherapy trial ever undertaken, which was conducted in the USA over a number of years, starting in 1989 (Project MATCH, 1997a, 1997b). This study, which compared three major and different methods of helping people with serious alcohol problems, all of which had good empirical support, showed that there were no major differences in how well people did, irrespective of which form of help they received. The three forms of help were Cognitive-Behavioural Therapy (CBT), Motivational Enhancement Therapy (MET), and 12-Step Facilitation (TSF).

But if most agencies and counsellors don't base their interventions on evidence, how do they decide on what sort of help to offer? Agencies and individuals differ in their philosophies and theories of the origins of problems; their counselling models; the techniques they use to intervene; the setting in which the intervention takes place; and the desired outcome of the intervention. There is no one set of key principles, methods, and techniques upon which all workers in the field will agree. If the counsellor believes his or her clients are 'alcoholics' or 'addicts', possessing some chemical imbalance where a taste of alcohol will automatically lead to uncontrollable misuse, then the solution they must recommend will be lifelong abstinence; if the counsellor believes the drink problem is a result of faulty learning experiences or inadequate coping strategies, then the counsellor's preferred solution will be for the client to relearn their method of drinking, or to develop more appropriate coping mechanisms. So what is offered is usually based more on counsellors' and agencies' philosophies and ideas than on the available evidence.

What is usually offered in the UK and the US?

Because there is no consensus as to the best way of dealing with alcohol-related problems, it is difficult to discuss the usual set of services clients will receive. However, in the time between the two editions of this book the dominant model in the UK has changed, from a medical/AA one, to a more individual, motivational, cognitive-behavioural, and counselling-focused approach.

Intervention in the medical/AA model generally revolves around some sort of formalized programme, into which all clients are expected to fit. After an initial assessment, clients are usually assigned a keyworker, who will take responsibility, and clarify which elements of the programme the client needs to attend. The programme normally consists of individual counselling sessions, groups (usually a range, including general alcohol education sessions, groups examining the effects of alcohol on clients' lives, and skills-based groups), and possibly occupational therapy activities. Many of these programmes have an explicit link with AA as well; often local members run internal AA groups or clients are referred to externally run AA groups, as a part of the programme.

Many such medical programmes utilize drug treatments as well, sometimes to reduce withdrawal effects (a benzodiazepine or Heminevrin); sometimes as a preventative measure (Antabuse or acamprosate or naltrexone); sometimes to reduce social anxiety (a benzodiazepine); and sometimes to help with clients' depression.

Occasionally, some of these programmes do not allow the use of any drug at all, even those prescribed for problems such as withdrawal or anxiety. This is because the belief underpinning the programmes is that some people are chemically dependent, and access to any drug will lead to that drug being substituted for the alcohol.

Intervention in the more individual, motivational, cognitive-behavioural, and counselling-focused approach revolves far more around one-to-one counselling, although many agencies do also utilize a variety of therapeutic groups. Many agencies also utilize the keyworker system, where one person co-ordinates all the elements of an individual's care.

In the US, the medical/disease approach is still very dominant, with strong AA links, alcohol education groups, group therapy, confrontation, Antabuse, and some individual counselling being used.

The perspective of this book

The approach adopted in this book is one drawn from a number of the approaches described in this and the previous chapter, but with strong leanings towards cognitive-behavioural, motivational, and client-focused counselling approaches. Four simple principles guide my thinking about drinking problems:

I believe that all *people do things for reasons*. It follows that people who drink too much have reasons for doing this as well. Most of us are not clearly aware of why we behave as we do, and clients are no different. It is our task as counsellors to help clients to understand their behaviour in order to empower them to change that behaviour.

Next, *dealing with individuals with alcohol problems involves addressing two distinct but related areas*, and counsellors will need to deal with both. One concerns the individual's use of drink *per se*; the second concerns other difficulties which connect in some way with the alcohol use. In the specialist field of alcohol counselling, it is often argued that if one deals with the alcohol, then the other problem areas will fall into place; or that if one deals with the other difficulties, for example housing, poverty, loneliness, the alcohol use will not be necessary, and hence will cease.

In fact, both are important. Individuals who misuse alcohol do so for reasons, some of which are not solely caused by the alcohol use. Yet it must also be recognized that alcohol is a drug which can produce considerable dependency, and this will usually lead to difficulty in giving up or cutting down, even if the reasons for the misuse are examined and successfully tackled. So both these areas must be examined, and discussions concerning what is 'the problem' should be avoided.

The next principle is that *counselling clients with alcohol problems is no different to any other type of counselling*. The counsellor working in this area needs to have both good general counselling skills, and specific knowledge about alcohol. Clients will often present with a range of problems besides alcohol misuse, and the counsellor needs to be able to address these issues as well. There are also problems connected with the alcohol use *per se*, and the counsellor will find it useful to have some particular, rather than general, knowledge. For example:

- How much alcohol is dangerous?
- What are the early signs of physical deterioration?
- How dangerous is it to mix alcohol with drugs prescribed to reduce withdrawal effects?
- How quickly should someone withdraw from alcohol?
- What is the best method of preventing relapse?
- How does one get a client to report accurately their alcohol use?

All these and other questions will regularly confront a counsellor working in these areas; it is important that the counsellor is familiar with the information he or she needs.

The final principle is that *it is not necessary for every counsellor who works with an alcohol-related problem to be a specialist counsellor.* Indeed, the number of people with drinking problems makes that an impossibility. A more sensible model would be for all or most counsellors to undergo some basic training orientated towards providing alcohol information. This would enable them to work – and feel confident about working – with alcohol-related issues as and when they arise.

And alcohol problems do arise in a variety of counselling settings. For example, many people attempt to cope with bereavement by drinking or taking drugs, and develop some sort of difficulty as a result. Such people may make their first contact with a bereavement counsellor. Also, alcohol is closely connected with marital violence and arguments; marriage guidance counsellors may be the first to see such clients. Young people are a target for much alcohol advertising, and youth counsellors may see many early problem drinkers.

Many clients who use agencies which do not specialize in alcohol counselling want to discuss their drinking and the related problems. This means that counsellors need to have general counselling skills, and also need to feel confident that they can apply them to the difficulty being presented. In turn, counsellors need to be informed about alcohol and related difficulties; it would be useful for them to know of techniques or skills that people who have worked in this field have used and found to be effective.

Besides these four principles, there are also a number of assumptions which I make in my work with people with alcohol problems.

Drinking and other behaviours, such as smoking, drug-taking, eating, and gambling, are all behaviours most people indulge in, but which for some people can become excessive and lead to problems. All such behaviours can be viewed along a continuum, from no or little use, through whatever might be considered normal by the society in which the individual lives, through to excessive usage. This firmly places the drinking of alcohol as a social phenomenon, where use occurs in relation to the socially approved norms of behaviour. It also, by introducing the concept of a continuum, breaks with the concept of alcoholics or addicts versus 'the rest'. This view is strongly counter to the type of medical or disease model described earlier; it does not hold that there is a diseased population which develops problems and a normal one which does not, but instead sees one population along a continuum.

Another assumption is that individuals can move on the continuum towards either of the extremes of excessive or limited use. This view has important implications for both prevention – how can we prevent people moving towards the problematic end? – and intervention – can we move people away from the problematic end? This also is in marked contrast to the disease model, which has few preventative implications (because one does not know who is going to become an alcoholic or an addict until they become one), and a simple intervention aim of total cessation of use.

Another assumption is that individuals learn how to behave with respect to alcohol, drugs, gambling, eating, and so on. As such, this learning can be analysed and modified. Chapters 4 and 5 include techniques based on the idea of modifying learnt patterns of behaviour.

The final assumption is that if people continue to use alcohol despite having developed problems as a result, there must be reasons for this, even if the individual is not aware of what these reasons are – the 'perpetuating factors' mentioned in Chapter 1.

Conclusion

This chapter has noted the many facilities providing help for problem drinkers in the UK and the US; indicated briefly the types of help offered; discussed some of the controversies concerned with the interventions provided; outlined the usual ways in which help is given; and described the approach of this book.

Key points

- Most people who develop problems related to their consumption of alcohol never receive any form of official or professional help. There are many reasons for this, but mostly it is because they find help and advice from family, friends and colleagues.
- For those who do turn to helping agencies, there exists a wide range providing help to people with drinking problems. Services are by volunteers, non-statutory agencies, statutory authorities, private bodies, and via workplaces.
- Services which might be offered include medical, individual counselling, group, and couple or family-orientated interventions.

- One sort of help is provided rather than another because of important differences between philosophies, theories of the cause of alcohol problems, preferred intervention and counselling methods, the setting, and the desired outcome.
- What is usually offered in the UK has changed over the past decade from a relatively fixed programme of intervention, often based at least partially on AA, to a more individually based counselling approach. The US is still dominated by a more disease/AA orientation.
- The perspective of this book is eclectic. It is based around four simple principles: people drink problematically for reasons; working with alcohol-misusing clients means we need to deal simultaneously with their alcohol use and other difficulties; counselling clients with these problems is no different to working with people with other types of difficulty; and it is not necessary to be a specialist counsellor to help clients with alcohol-related problems.
- Additional assumptions include: alcohol use lies along a continuum – there is no simple dividing line between alcoholic drinkers and the rest of the population; individuals can move along this continuum, in either direction; individuals learn how to behave towards alcohol, and this is open to change; if people continue to use alcohol despite developing problems, this must occur for reasons.

References and further reading

Alcohol Concern (1997) *Alcohol Services Directory: Services for Problem Drinkers in England and Wales.* London: Dolomite Publishing.

Cameron, D. (1995) *Liberating Solutions to Alcohol Problems.* London: Jason Aronson Inc.

Cooper, D. (1994) *Alcohol Home Detoxification and Assessment.* Edinburgh: Radcliffe Medical Press.

Davidson, R., Rofinick, S. and MacEwan, I. (eds) (1991) *Counselling Problem Drinkers.* London: Routledge.

Edwards, G., Marshall, E. and Cook, C. (1997) *The Treatment of Drinking Problems: a Guide for the Helping Professions* (3rd edn). Cambridge: Cambridge University Press.

Heather, N. and Robertson, I. (1997) *Problem Drinking: the New Approach* (3rd edn). Oxford: Oxford University Press.

Miller, W., Andrews, N., Wilbourne, P. and Bennett, M. (1998) 'A wealth of alternatives: effective treatments for alcohol problems', in W. Miller and N. Heather (eds), *Treating Addictive Behaviour* (2nd edn). New York: Plenum Press.

Orford, J. (2001) *Excessive Appetites* (2nd edn). Chichester: Wiley.

Orford, J. and Edwards, G. (1977) *Alcoholism: a Comparison of Treatment and Advice, with a Study of the Influence of Marriage.* Oxford: Oxford University Press.

Pattison, E., Sobell, M. and Sobell, L. (1977) *Emerging Concepts of Alcohol Dependency*. New York: Springer.

Project MATCH Research Group (1997a) 'Matching alcoholism treatments to client heterogeneity: Project MATCH post-treatment drinking outcomes', *Journal of Studies on Alcohol*, 58: 7–29.

Project MATCH Research Group (1997b) 'Project MATCH secondary a priori hypotheses', *Addiction*, 92: 1671–98.

Sobell, M. and Sobell, L. (1978) *Behavioral Treatment of Alcohol Problems. Individualized Therapy and Controlled Drinking*. New York: Plenum.

Velleman, R. (1991) 'Alcohol and drug problems', in W. Dryden and R. Rentoul (eds), *Clinical Problems: a Cognitive-Behavioural Approach*. London: Sage.

Velleman, R. (1997) 'Counselling people with alcohol and drug problems', in S. Palmer and G. McMahon (eds), *The Handbook of Counselling* (2nd edn). London: Routledge.

PART 2

HELPING PEOPLE WITH ALCOHOL PROBLEMS

3

The Process of Counselling and the Cycle of Change

C ounselling clients with alcohol-related problems is both similar to and different from counselling clients with any other problems. This chapter deals with the features which are similar.

First I will underline the general approach I advocate in this book. It is very simple: I believe that we should work with the clients who come to us for help, seeking to empower them so they can feel responsible for the changes they will have to make. Our task is not to tell clients what they should do.

Anyone who has practised as a counsellor will be familiar with this idea, yet it is often undermined. New counsellors often feel it is their duty to give advice. It is not. In most cases the task of counselling is to draw out the client and enable him or her to reach a greater level of understanding, or a greater commitment to take action.

Another reason for wanting to tell clients what to do is that many counsellors possess exactly the attributes needed to be good counsellors! Effective counsellors need to be empathic – to pick up on the meanings which underpin the things our clients tell us, and to gain a deep understanding of them. It will thus often happen that we feel we know exactly what the client should/ought/must do in order for him or her to start or continue to change: if only the client would do 'x', then lots of other things would fall into place; the temptation is very strong for us to say 'If I were you, I'd . . .' or 'What you've got to do is . . .'.

While it is impossible always to resist these feelings, such an intervention runs counter to the approach of this book, which suggests that clients will be far more likely to change, and this change is far more likely to be maintained, if *they* decide to make the change, and if *they* decide what that change is going to be. If we as counsellors direct our clients' choices, they can easily interpret these decisions as being ours, not theirs. This in turn can lead to them being less committed to making or maintaining any changes.

This does not mean we can never make suggestions to clients, who will often need help and hints to get them thinking. However, how we make these suggestions is all-important. Enabling clients to realize that alternatives exist, and helping them to clarify what some of those choices are, is a key part of counselling.

Counselling and change

There are two processes which co-exist: the process of counselling, which underpins what we do as counsellors; and the process of change, which underpins what our clients do. This chapter will look at them in turn – first the counselling process, and then the change process.

The process of counselling

A number of writers (most notably Egan, an American psychologist) argue that, irrespective of its theoretical model, counselling must go through various stages if it is to be successful. People suggest various numbers of stages: my own view is that conceptualizing counselling as having six stages is the most useful:

- developing trust;
- exploring problem areas;
- helping to set goals;
- empowering into action;
- helping to maintain change;
- agreeing when to end.

These stages of counselling apply to all problem areas, and are just as important for the client with alcohol-related problems as they are for any other client.

What this 'process model' does is to pull together various concepts developed over the years, for example:

- the value of warmth, genuineness, and empathy (the 'developing-trust' stage);

- the ideas which psychoanalysts and behaviourists see as central: the clear and deep analysis of what the problem is, where it comes from, why it has developed (the 'exploring-the-problem' stage);
- the importance of goal-directed interventions, which behavioural and cognitive-behavioural theorists introduced (the 'goal-setting' stage);
- the need for action to achieve goals, again introduced by behaviourists and cognitive-behaviourists, and also by other psychotherapeutic schools such as Gestalt (the 'action' stage);
- the importance of support and other techniques to enable clients to maintain changes, stressed by many;
- and the emphasis on the whole process being directed by the client rather than the counsellor.

I shall briefly examine each of these stages.

The stages of counselling

Stage one – developing trust
The essential point about this stage is that if it is not successfully completed, all other attempts at counselling will be ineffectual. *Trust is the underpinning of all counselling relationships, and of all counselling stages.*

The prospective client often arrives in a concerned frame of mind – 'Do I want to be here?' 'What do they do here?' 'What will they expect of me?' 'What is "counselling"?' 'Will I finish in time to pick the children up from school?' 'Am I going mad?' He or she will often be worried, uncertain, anxious, angry, defensive, and so on. This negative frame of mind is particularly common in clients with alcohol-related difficulties because not being able to control one's alcohol use is seen as a sign of lack of willpower, and as an indication of 'weakness'; being an 'alcoholic' is seen in very negative ways by many people. Many clients will know from past experience that many agencies reject clients with alcohol problems, preferring not to work with them.

Something will have made the client come for help at this particular time, such as worrying news from a doctor; comments – or instructions or an ultimatum – from a spouse or an employer; a television programme about sensible drinking. They will therefore come uncertain whether or not they might be damaging their health; or worried that they might be an 'alcoholic' – having all the negative stereotypes most of the general public have about those with drinking problems.

Once we meet the client, other worrying questions will emerge: 'What does the counsellor think of me?' 'I need specific information – will they have it?' Our job as counsellors is to alter such anxious thoughts so that instead the client is thinking: 'What a relief to talk to somebody' 'S/he seems to understand me' 'S/he seems to know what s/he's talking about.'

If we can successfully show our clients that we are people who can be trusted, who will take them seriously, listening to and understanding their problems, doubts, fears, and aspirations, then they will feel positive about seeing us, and will be more likely to come back.

The problem is that, like the client, we as counsellors have concerns too, especially if we are new or if we are insecure with a particular client or type of client. The counsellor's concerns may include: 'Can I help?' 'Am I talking too little, or too much?' 'Am I in control?' 'Am I good enough?' 'Do I know enough?' 'What does the client think of me?'

Some of these concerns will decrease as we become more experienced in counselling, and more experienced in counselling problem drinkers. Shaw and his colleagues (1977) suggested that counsellors will only work with problem drinkers, and will only develop the skills needed to work with them, if they feel secure, which in turn will emerge only if they feel supported by other workers experienced in the field.

But even after such security is reached, some concerns will always remain. For example, I still feel both excited and anxious every time I meet a new client: excited because I am going to confront a new problem and learn about a new person; and anxious because even after years of seeing clients I am not sure whether or not I will be able to help with the fresh challenges which are about to be presented.

It is important to remember the limits as well as the possibilities of what can be achieved. The initial counselling session(s) provide a place and a time for the client to take advantage of the help being offered, so it is all right for the client to ask for help; it provides us with an opportunity to offer warmth, concern, understanding, encouragement, and hope; we are prepared to begin to understand the client's difficulties from the client's point of view.

We communicate these possibilities by how we act towards our clients. The skills we use to develop trust include:

- listening, and showing we are listening;
- showing respect by looking interested, creating the space for the client to talk, and by not interrupting;
- reflecting both the verbal and emotional content of what has been said;
- asking for clarifications, and focusing, which enables the client to be specific;
- allowing silences;
- demonstrating warmth, understanding, and genuineness by the use of non-verbal behaviour, such as nods, the use of our hands, our posture, by what we say, and the way we say it;
- summarizing by expressing briefly and simply the difficulty the client has described, and asking the client whether or not that is correct.

We can also develop trust by making explicit some of the goals that perhaps can be achieved in the counselling session; telling the client how much time there is, what the agency does, what counselling is, how many sessions we might offer; allowing time at the end of the session to look at what has been covered, what is possible, in order to offer hope and to plan for future sessions, if they are wanted.

Case example – Harry
Early in my first session with Harry (see page 1), I said something along the lines of:

- 'This is a one-off session for us to start to get to know each other, and to see whether or not you feel I might be able to help.'
- 'At the end, we'll discuss whether or not you want to see me again.'
- 'If you do, we'll meet for, say, five sessions, and spend the fifth session with you reviewing what you have got from the sessions so far, what work remains to be done, and whether you want to do it with me or move on.'

This let Harry know that this first session was an exploratory one, to see whether or not he liked my way of working. At the end of the first session he said he wanted to continue, and so we arranged a series of five more.

Not only do such statements provide a structure and frame-work for the client early on – so they can understand the first session and how it might fit into subsequent sessions – but being open about the agenda helps the development of trust, which is essential.

Stage two – exploring the problem

Because clients often arrive for counselling feeling confused, we must help them to clarify exactly what the problem is with which they want help – or, more likely, the range of problems. The sorts of questions which should be in our minds during this exploration phase include the following:

What is the problem they are initially coming with? In this case, it will probably be connected with drinking, but possibly not directly so: it could be the arguments with the spouse that drinking is leading to. Irrespective of what the initially presented problem is, we should always be aiming to get a clear understanding of its dimensions: what, when, where, with whom, for how long, with what intensity, and over what period. For example:

- 'What' might be a severe anxiety or panic attack.
- 'When' might be mid-morning, most days.
- 'Where' might be at home.
- 'With whom' might be when the client is on his or her own.
- 'How long' might be 'For ten minutes, which feels like a lifetime.'
- 'Intensity' might be severe: 'I feel like I am dying.'
- 'Time period' might be 'For the last month, which is why I've decided to come and see someone for help.'

What other problems are caused by or help maintain the presenting problem? For example, if someone presents with a drinking problem, it is important to help the client to clarify how this is affecting his or her life in other ways – relationships, friendships, social life, job and finances.

What long-standing, or underlying, problems are around? Often during exploration, or later, issues start to emerge which have a repetitive feel to them – clients will report having had similar problems in previous relationships, for example; or the client will tell us he or she thinks certain current problems are related to past issues, connected, perhaps, to his/her relationship with a parent.

All this is clarifying, for both the client and us, what the problem actually is. Almost certainly the picture will be complicated – if it was not, the client would have worked it out long ago – but the more information is gleaned, the more likely it is the picture will become clearer – for us, and, more importantly, for the client.

There are certain areas which should not be lost sight of in exploration and after:

- Thoughts – what is our client saying to him/herself, both in the session and outside of it?
- Feelings – what emotions are present, and how are these affecting both what is said or done in and out of the session and the extent to which our client can listen to this session?
- Behaviour – how is our client behaving, both in the session and outside?
- Unconscious elements – what might be going on about which our client might not be aware, and can we help to bring such things into awareness? For example, 'It struck me that there are a lot of similarities between the way you describe your wife and the feelings you still have about your father – do you think that they might be connected?'
- Life events – all the above are internal; but external events must also be taken into account. These range from a train being late, through to a serious bereavement.
- Life stages – there are certain points in people's lives when particular problems are to be expected: examinations, marriage, births, early stages of child-rearing, retirement.
- External pressures and constraints – other external issues may affect people's ability to move and change: attitudes of family, work colleagues, friends, financial issues, and so on.

The emphasis on each of these elements will vary depending on which theoretical position is held, but each matters, and some will be more important with some clients than with others.

The defining and clarifying of problems does not occur in isolation, to be covered in the first and second sessions for example. Clients will gradually give us more information about themselves, and with our help will continue to learn more about themselves. In the same way that trust continues to grow over the whole of the counselling relationship, so exploration continues.

Another point that needs to be borne in mind during the exploration stage – as well as during all other stages – is that exploration is conducted for the client's benefit, not the counsellor's. This means that the above questions and areas are not to be used as a checklist, to be slavishly gone through in the first or second interview so as to 'assess' the client. The idea is to help the client to understand him or herself by clarifying the range and intensity of the various problem areas, which will reduce the sense of confusion and of having lost control with which so many clients arrive.

It is then possible for the client, helped by the counsellor, to move on to the next stage of setting goals.

Exploration helps the client to gain new perspectives on their problems. The sorts of skills we use to enable clients to do this are questioning, listening, and linking; other skills include:

- giving information: 'Often people who want to control their drinking . . .'; or 'Some people who drink too much have found it helpful to . . .'; or 'People going through a divorce often find that . . .'
- displaying a deeper empathy: sharing 'hunches', stating things that are not explicitly expressed ('There appears to be a sadness there'); connecting themes; 'reframing' events or issues.
- helping the client to go deeper by identifying themes, asking the client to draw conclusions from what they have said so far.

Yet other skills may involve confronting the client more directly with issues which may be uncomfortable:

- directly confronting issues that arise in the session: sometimes clients seem only to talk about their negative sides; or seem to hold very self-defeating beliefs which keep them from moving forwards, and these need to be responsibly and carefully challenged.
- using our own discomfort, or negative feelings: 'I'm feeling a bit uncomfortable at the moment because . . .'; or 'I'm feeling confused. I thought you were saying that . . . but now I seem to be hearing the opposite.'
- engaging the client in a mutual exercise: 'There seems to be . . . between us at the moment; what do you think?'

Having gained a new perspective and been helped to see the problem in a different light, the client is left with the question, 'OK, but what now?' If nothing follows, the client will often feel worse: 'I understand better, but I still haven't changed' – and if that happens, stagnation and disappointment often follow. Instead, we must help the client to move onwards from the new perspective, by helping them to set goals. Knowledge – of what the problems are and why they occur – on its own, without the ability to change or to manage these problems better, can be damaging.

Case example – Harry

I had given Harry (see pp. 1 and 36) the space in the first session to start to tell me how he felt about himself, his bereavement, and his drinking. He trusted me sufficiently by the end of the session to return. The developing trust in the counselling relationship allowed us to move into a deeper exploratory phase.

He began to see that his heavy drinking was a far more long-standing problem than he had initially realized, or was prepared to reveal; and he recalled that his wife had wished him to cut down long before she died. This in turn exposed his guilt about having failed her, which had contributed to his inability to adequately resolve his grief, and to stop his even heavier drinking since her death.

Gaining this new perspective without enabling Harry to move on and change his behaviour could have been counter-productive: he would have better understood his negative feeling for himself; he would have broken down many of his defences, which he had put up to protect himself from the pain of his guilt as well as of his bereavement – but he would still not know in what direction to change, or how to effect that change.

Stage three – helping clients set their own goals

What are goals? They are aims, intentions, ends towards which the client is moving; purposes, ambitions, and targets. Goals should be:

- specific and clear (S);
- measurable and verifiable (M);
- adequate to meet the problem (A);
- realistic and achievable (R);
- timely (i.e. set in the right time range) (T);
- in the client's control;
- in line with the client's values.

The first five of these are often known under the acronym SMART (as in 'you need SMART goals' or 'goals should be SMART'), to which I have added two relating to my focus on counselling's central role in empowering our clients.

One problem which often besets clients is TINA, or 'There Is No Alternative'. Clients often get stuck by convincing themselves that only one course of action, or one goal, is possible. Often the goal which they argue is the only valid one is in fact impossible to achieve, which totally immobilizes them: they want to move, but the only way to do so is closed to them.

For example, a client who is drinking 140 units per week might insist on stopping immediately, painlessly, permanently, and with no medication – without considering alternatives such as cutting down, or using medication to reduce withdrawal effects. Harry, for example, might argue that there is no way he can stop drinking without dealing first with his guilt at failing his wife – but he cannot deal with that because she is dead.

Much of this stage of counselling is taken up with teaching clients TAAA, or 'There Are Always Alternatives'. Much of goal-setting and action consists of helping clients to see there are alternatives to every course of action, and of helping them to work out what some of the alternatives are.

Goal-setting moves on from exploration. Having clarified the range of problems which beset the client, we help him or her to select the one problem area he or she wants to work on first, because it is the most important, or the most worrying or upsetting, or the easiest to make progress on. The decision must be the client's, not the counsellor's. In one sense this is an impossible task, as most of a client's problems are interrelated. It is not possible in most cases, however, to help clients to solve all their problems simultaneously, so a start has to be made somewhere.

It is crucial in this situation to dispense with dogmatic attitudes. Many counsellors start to work with problem drinkers believing that if one solves the alcohol problem, all the other problems will 'fall into place'; other counsellors hold the opposite view, believing that if the non-drinking problems are solved, the drinking will solve itself.

Both views are based on a theoretical position about the 'cause' of alcohol problems. While either view may be 'correct' in an individual case, it is not for the counsellor to decide this. The task of selecting which problem to start with is the client's, although it is our job to try to ensure that the goals are realistic. It is vital to focus on both the alcohol elements, and the non-alcohol elements; both will need to be tackled at some stage in counselling.

Having decided on the problem to be tackled first, we then help the client to clarify medium- and short-term goals. The medium-term goals can be elicited in a number of ways. One is to use the future tense: 'In a year's time, I will be able to do . . . or I will be feeling . . .'. So, for example, a client might say that in a year's time he or she wants to be consuming no alcohol at all; or to be consuming less than 10 units per week; or that he or she wants to be having a much improved relationship with a spouse; or to have moved to a different sort of accommodation.

Another way is to get the client to brainstorm a variety of possible goals or outcomes open to him or her – by directly asking, by suggesting as a trigger, by summarizing, and so on. Often a client will hold the view that no options exist, for example, 'I can't afford the mortgage, so I shall have to leave.' The focus of this stage is to enable the client to realize that there are a huge number of alternatives, that a choice between them can be made, and that each option has both advantages and disadvantages.

Having clarified some of the medium-term aims, the general aims need to be made more specific. For example, if an aim is to 'improve the quality of my relationship with my son', this needs to be refined into, say, 'I want to have more equal conversations without them deteriorating into arguments', which in turn can become the more specific goal of, 'Over the next two weeks I shall cut by half the number of times I have conversations with my son which deteriorate into arguments.' This is based on the assumption that in the exploration phase we have clarified how often the problem – in this case having conversations which deteriorate into arguments – occurs: if we do not know the rate of conversations-into-arguments, we cannot assess whether or not the rate has halved.

So, goal-setting involves:

- clarifying the medium-term goals;
- choosing one goal to work on;
- making that goal more specific.

Skills used at this stage include:

- asking;
- summarizing;
- brainstorming;
- suggesting as a trigger;
- balancing (getting the client to think of the advantages and disadvantages of each option).

Case example – Harry

One way to get clients to think about medium-to-long-term goals is to ask them to write an account of their lives in, say, five years' time, given an ideal world where most things are possible. The account has to be relatively full, including where they are living, with whom, what they do during the day, how they spend their leisure time, and so on.

Such an account provides a framework for goal-setting in a number of areas, and forces the client to confront possibly radical changes in many aspects of their lives. Once these medium-term goals are decided upon, one can move on to considering action quite quickly: if you want to be able to do this in five years' time, what must your life look like in four years' time? If it is going to look like that in three years, what must be happening in two years? This means that you must be doing 'a' in six months, which means that you must be doing 'b' in three months, 'c' in one month, 'd' in two weeks. So in order to get to your long-term goal in five years' time, you need to do 'e' within the next week.

When Harry and I carried out this task, he realized he had a number of short- and long-term goals. For example, he wished to abstain completely from drinking alcohol; to rebuild his relationship with his older daughter; to enable his younger daughter, who seemed to spend much of her time looking after him, to develop a life of her own; to re-start his social life, and so on.

Stage four – empowering into action

Action is the next stage in a process that started long before the first encounter between us and the client:

- Before coming for counselling, something happened which led to a change in attitude.
- The client came and met the counsellor.
- Trust developed.
- Communication occurred.
- This created a feeling of relief.
- The client and counsellor explored the issues together.
- The client felt clearer.
- He or she set goals.
- This led to the client feeling more positive about the need to change these things in his or her life.

While setting goals can make people feel more hopeful about the future, acting on those goals involves doing something, and this is difficult for many people. Changing behaviour may lead to positive outcomes, but it also involves taking risks (e.g. the risk of failing); and continuing to feel positive (i.e. to have confidence) requires being able to see results from action.

The way forward is to have a plan of action wherein the client, supported by the counsellor, moves towards the agreed goal in stages using achievable subgoals so that the process of learning and self-development can go on. For this to occur, we and the client need to work out a route for achieving the goal which takes into account both opportunities and pitfalls. Even though the alternatives produced by the brainstorming exercise need not always be realistic, the final strategy and action plan must be realistic.

Having clarified the medium- and short-term goals, the next step is empowering the client to take action. Deciding on the goal does not clarify how the client can put it into action, which is done by planning with the client a detailed strategy.

For example, if the goal is 'Cut down my drinking to two pints a week', we might work out with the client that the strategy between now and next week might be 'To only go out with my wife in the evening; not to go to pubs frequented by my drinking friends; only to take sufficient money with me for two rounds of drinks', and so on.

An important idea to get across to the client at this stage is that these strategies are not necessarily the correct ones. The client and counsellor do not know what the right thing to do is – if the client did, he or she would have done it already, and if we knew, we would be fortune-tellers, not counsellors! The client has to realize that the campaign is a testing out of some ideas, which may or may not work. The vital thing is the testing of the ideas in practice, and then discussing how well or otherwise the ideas have worked. If they do not work, it is not a failure, but simply provides more information which we and the client can assess together and use to create a further strategic plan.

Such a strategy informs the subsequent meetings with the client, in which we evaluate the success or otherwise of the chosen course of action. If successful, we and the client move on to a further course of action, or choose another problem area and repeat the process. If unsuccessful, we explore why, and then help to set courses of action which will not suffer from the same problems, for example by choosing a course of action that involves a smaller or less threatening change, or one that has contingency plans built into it.

Throughout this process the client should be learning to:

- collaborate and co-operate;
- make his or her own decisions;
- become better at risk-taking;
- reshape and re-create his or her future;
- accept responsibility for his or her actions;
- evaluate what he or she is doing.

Besides the previous ones described, the skills we use in this action phase include the following.

BRAINSTORMING TO GET OPTIONS   The rules for brainstorming are: suspend judgement, encourage quantity, allow fun or silly ideas to emerge, encourage lateral thinking. Use questions such as, 'Who/what can help you? Where? When?' Aim for quantity.

APPRAISING   List the advantages and disadvantages, gains and costs, for the self and significant others, of each option.

STRATEGY PLANNING   Help the client to work out the steps in a detailed action plan, with contingency plans. For example, if the goal is to go out together in the evening to have just two drinks, the plan might be:
   Step 1 – 'Get a reliable babysitter, but if we can't, use the contingency plan: we'll go out for the day on a family railcard and have a drink in a family pub with the baby at lunchtime. Then neither of us will go out in the evening.' Then return to the appraisal stage, and question whether or not the contingency plan is better than the original. Or 'If the babysitter doesn't turn up, the contingency plan is . . .'.
   Step 2 – 'I'll only take enough money for two rounds of drinks – but if someone offers me a further drink, I'll . . .', and so on.

BALANCING   Examine facilitating and restraining forces which will help or hinder the plan – support from others, money, craving, danger times, past successes and failures, being let down. Work with the client to reduce restrainers and strengthen facilitators.

EVALUATING   Check especially:

- the quality of client participation – is the client really committed to the chosen plan and goal?
- the quality of the action programme – is it working, or does it need amending?
- the quality of the goals – are they actually dealing with the issues, or do they need to be changed?

One useful way I use to conceptualize the process of exploration, goal-setting, and action is to see this as a constant process of expansion and contraction. In exploring the problem we are expanding the range of problem areas we are talking about; in goal-setting we contract to one problem area which we are going to work on; we then:

- expand to delineate a number of goals;
- contract so that one goal is chosen;
- expand that goal to a number of more specific goals;
- contract to one specific goal to be worked on;
- expand by brainstorming all the ways to achieve that goal;
- contract to choose one preferred option;
- expand to plan with the client a detailed strategy of exactly how he or she will put the plan into action.

Stage five – helping to maintain change

Although for many people working through the myriad issues surrounding a major change in behaviour is time-consuming and difficult, once the decision to change has been taken, doing this is relatively easy. Ask anyone who has stopped smoking. Most will say that once they had decided to stop, the actual stopping (for the first day or half-day) was relatively easy. The difficult part was staying stopped. The same issue arises with dieting – most people can stick to their diet for a day or two; it is sticking to it week in, week out that is difficult.

How can we help clients to maintain changes? Two replies emerge: first, clients need support after taking action; second, clients need to learn specific skills, which will often be different from the skills they used to take the action in the first place.

SUPPORT   Making changes in our lives is often difficult and painful. The relationship a client has developed with us has enabled him or her to start to change; but changing fundamental ways of behaving, thinking, or interacting is unlikely to happen all at once. It is more likely that many difficulties will occur, providing opportunities for the client to regress to his or her original problematic behaviour. The relationship which has enabled the progress so far will be important in enabling the client to cope with these demands.

SKILLS CLIENTS NEED   There are a variety of skills the client may need either to learn or to utilize in order to enable him or her to keep the desired changes going.

As well as the support of the counsellor, a key issue in counselling is helping clients to develop their own support networks outside of the counselling relationship so that they need us less. For example, clients may need help in developing the skills to make and maintain new friendships, possibly through attendance at a social skills group, or they may need to brainstorm ideas of where to meet people.

Having learnt the skills to deal with a problem in the short term, many clients need help dealing with longer-term issues, when motivation is flagging and skills such as anxiety management are less useful. Clients almost invariably need to alter aspects of their lifestyles. For example, if their drinking has revolved around the pub, clients may have to develop new, or expand existing, interests. In the useful booklet *Helping Problem Drinkers*, Ward (1988) suggests that one way of dealing with these longer-term difficulties is to work through three questions with the client:

- 'Which are the situations where I find it hard to avoid having a drink, and which are the ones where I find it easy? Can I increase the situations which are easy?'
- 'What alternatives are there to my drinking? Which of these will I try?'
- 'What is my drinking goal this week? What will I change this week? How will I reward myself if I succeed?'

Stage six – ending counselling

Ideally, counselling ends when the client has successfully worked through the various goals he or she, with our help, has delineated. When the client has acted on these goals, and the action has been successful and maintained, the client is ready to move on.

Unfortunately, ending counselling is often not so simple for at least two reasons. The first is that the process of exploration, goal-setting, and action is never-ending: there are always new goals to be striven for. Hence, counselling ends not when all the goals have been realized, but when clients have mastered the process they must go through in order to translate problems into solutions that can be acted upon and maintained. Counselling ends when the client can do what goes on in counselling without our help.

Counselling can be seen as an activity that has two functions: to enable the client to learn the skills of exploring, goal-setting, action, and maintenance; and to support the client through the difficult process of change. When the client can continue to work on the problems on his or her own without our questioning, and when he or she has sufficient support from people other than us, then we can gradually decrease our input.

The second reason why ending counselling is not so simple is that the counselling relationship we have built up can itself contribute difficulties during this gradual running-down process.

Clients often become very involved with us, and may come to feel dependent upon us. Sometimes clients relapse or develop new problems in order to retain the counselling relationship. Sometimes, also, we as counsellors become attached to our clients, and may find it difficult to give them up. This can lead to a counsellor continually finding new issues which need resolution before the client is 'really ready' to face life independently. Often the dependency is mutual – counsellor and client interact to retain the relationship. Many of these client/counsellor issues will need to be brought to the supervisory relationship; this is discussed below.

Summary and overview

The six stages of trust, exploration, goal-setting, action, maintenance, and ending describe the process that we will go through with all clients. Of course, it is not as clearly defined as the preceding pages make out – for example, we might pass through a number of stages in a single interview; or any one stage – especially the second – might take longer than the others. The process is cyclical in that the action stage will almost certainly throw up new information, which will inform the whole plan we and the client have made together, and will therefore serve as a further part of the exploration phase. Problems connected with taking action, therefore, will provide exploratory material, may cause us to revise the goals, and will influence the taking of further action.

Case example – Harry

Harry developed the goal that he wanted to abstain from drinking altogether. The two of us worked out a plan of action for the forthcoming week to enable him to do this, with the major thrust coming from Harry rather than from me: we identified possible at-risk situations and we clarified the strategies and tactics he was going to employ so as to successfully overcome these.

The next week, Harry returned saying he had failed: he had drunk four units of alcohol. He was out with one of his adult daughters, they went for a country walk, and ended up in a pub for lunch. He had two pints with his meal, then continued with his walk, and had drunk nothing else throughout the week.

This information was used in a variety of ways. It added more material which was useful for exploration – Harry can successfully control his intake under some circumstances, drinking four units did not precipitate a full-scale relapse, and so on. It also provided the possibility for reassessing the goals – perhaps some drinking, under controlled and monitored conditions, with certain people and in certain contexts might be a desired goal? This new material altered the plan of campaign for the next and subsequent weeks.

If abstinence was still the goal, new at-risk situations had been identified, and new strategies had to be developed to overcome them, i.e. do not go for walks, or take a packed lunch, or stop in a village with a café, or get his daughter to buy the (non-alcoholic) drinks, or get her to hold the money.

Alternatively, if occasional controlled drinking was now the goal, the details of when, how much, with whom, where, and so on needed to be clarified; risky situations relating to these actions needed to be identified; and strategies to overcome them needed to be thought through – with, as always, the major thrust coming from Harry rather than me.

Skills and behaviour

Skills

The range of skills that can be used at each stage is broad. A number of books and teaching packs are available that cover these areas in more detail. Some of these are noted at the end of this chapter, but particularly useful and recommended guides are those by Egan (1990) and Inskipp (1986).

Behaviour

So far we have concentrated on the process of counselling, arguing that we use the same processes in counselling clients with alcohol-related problems as we do in counselling anyone else. Another general point concerns the importance of behaviour.

The most fundamental thing is to help the client to change his or her behaviour. With alcohol problems one might be able to help the client to alter his or her thoughts about the drinking, or feelings about the drinking, but until the client decides to behave differently, the problem is likely to remain unresolved.

The three elements that are central to helping clients to change their behaviour are performance, practice, and homework.

PERFORMANCE   Although clients' attitudes, ideas and wishes need to be examined and addressed, talking on its own is unlikely to provide all the help. There must be a behavioural (performance) component to the intervention as well: people must *do* something different about their problematic behaviour, as well as talk about it.

PRACTISE OR REHEARSAL   The issue of practise arises because helping a client to change his or her behaviour will almost certainly involve the development of new skills, and as with any new skills, these must be practised.

HOMEWORK   Some of the practise will occur in the counselling sessions, but much of it will occur in the client's outside life and will relate to the client's behaviour, relationships, social networks, and community within which his or her alcohol problems are enacted. Hence it is important to negotiate with the client some task(s) which he or she will carry out during the times between the sessions. As a general rule, these tasks must not be too many or too ambitious: failure is a bad learning experience. The tasks will usually involve the client practising some of the skills or strategies discussed in the session.

Supervision and support

Counselling people often feels difficult:

- We may put a lot into it, yet the client may still not change.
- The client may say things which link into our own problems and conflicts.
- We may feel unskilled sometimes due to the particular difficulties a client brings.
- We may lose our way, and be unsure where to go next.
- We may develop a cosy relationship with a client such that we meet regularly and talk well together without realizing that the sessions are drifting with little focus, and that we are failing to help the client to move on.

For exactly these reasons, most agencies insist on counsellors receiving frequent and high-quality supervision, and most national organizations require it before granting accreditation to counsellors. So, for example, the British Association for Counselling includes in its *Code of Ethics and Practice* a variety of standards to which counsellors are expected to conform, including 'counsellors monitor their counselling work through regular supervision by professionally competent supervisors and are able to account to clients and colleagues for what they do and why'.

What is supervision?

Alcohol Concern (1991, 1992a, 1992b) states that supervision has a number of characteristics:

- *It is formal*. It is not ad hoc, or a chat when we feel like it, or when there happens to be someone around with the time (in busy agencies there is often very little of that!). It is a scheduled time with a supervisor who has been selected because he or she has the skills and experience to be able to offer a high-quality service.
- *It is regular*. If we see a number of clients on a regular basis, issues will certainly arise which need to be dealt with. Alcohol Concern insists on one hour of supervision for every four of counselling, and for many full-time counsellors that would prove to be a very demanding degree of regularity. Whatever the frequency decided by the agency, regularity must be ensured.
- The supervision *provides an opportunity* for the counsellor *to develop and explore* in a number of ways, including to:

  - develop the skills and understanding of his or her counselling work;
  - develop self-awareness, in so far as this affects the quality of the counselling work;
  - explore counselling issues and difficulties for counsellor or clients as they arise in sessions;
  - provide protection for the client and the agency by monitoring the counsellor's work.

These characteristics imply that supervision should be taken up with a number of tasks. Supervisors should utilize the same process model that is so useful in counselling itself, as outlined below.

Effective support and supervision is based on trust. The counsellor must feel able to disclose things during supervision which he or she might not tell other people – for example, feelings of incompetence, mistakes made, annoyance with the agency.

The supervisor needs to explore what the issues and concerns are that a counsellor has, rather than imagining he or she knows what those concerns are.

The supervisor needs to help the counsellor focus on the issues, rather than skirting around the edges. For example, many supervisors allow the counsellor to recount, at great length, the case history which the counsellor has painstakingly extracted from the client – as opposed to getting the counsellor to focus on the issues that this client has thrown up for him or her. The supervisor could examine these by asking questions such as, 'What are you actually doing with this client?' 'What are your plans?' 'What are the difficulties which have emerged for you in the sessions so far?' Or the supervisor might focus on the counsellor's understanding of the problem as opposed to his or her goals; or focus on the counsellor's feelings for the client and how these might interact with the work which is being attempted.

The supervisor needs to help the counsellor to take action in a counselling session by helping him or her to plan out how to implement the strategies and ideas which have emerged during the supervision meeting.

Who should supervise?

Supervisors are people who are experienced counsellors. This is generally a positive thing, because they will be familiar with many of the issues that are likely to confront counsellors. But it can also lead to problems. One is that many supervisors have had little training offered to them on how to supervise. Being a good counsellor does not necessarily mean the person can supervise. The second problem is that counsellors are interested in clients, which is why they counsel. Supervisors chosen because of their counselling experience and interest can easily get waylaid into becoming more interested in the clients who are being talked about than in the counsellor, who needs to develop better ways of understanding and dealing with their clients.

Alcohol Concern has laid down minimum standards of qualification and experience for supervisors of voluntary counsellors. They must have: *either* completed counsellor training, or a professional qualification that includes training in counselling, and also have a minimum of two years' experience of using their counselling skills; *or* been counselling for a minimum of five years, with supervision. Alcohol Concern has also issued guidelines (1992b) that describe in more detail how to supervise effectively.

The cycle of change

The six stages of counselling – the process of counselling – are important. However, another interesting idea has been introduced into the alcohol counselling world over the last two decades – the 'cycle of change'. Two American psychologists, Prochaska and DiClemente, initially produced their model from the work they had done with people wishing to change their smoking behaviour. It soon became clear that their theory was helpful for all the addictive behaviours: alcohol, drugs, over-eating, gambling, and so on. I think these ideas are useful in counselling generally, and that clients with all sorts of problems go through the 'cycle of

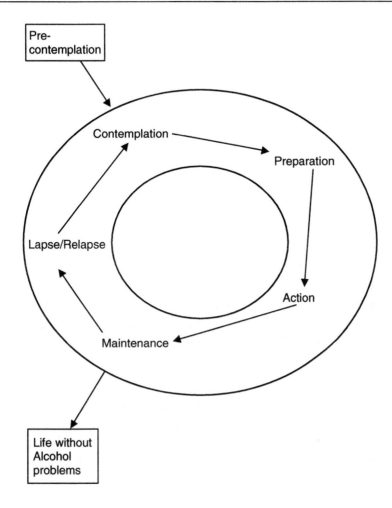

Figure 3.1 *The Prochaska and DiClemente cycle of change*

change' in the same way that people with alcohol-related problems do. Steve Rollnick, Pip Mason and Chris Butler agree: their
excellent book incorporates this approach into work across all the
'health behaviour change' areas (Rollnick et al., 1999).

Prochaska and DiClemente first published their ideas in 1983,
and these have been updated over the years (DiClemente and
Prochaska, 1998). They showed that when clients arrive for counselling, they may be at one of a variety of stages, each of which
they gave a name to. These are displayed diagrammatically in
Figure 3.1.

PRE-CONTEMPLATION STAGE   Here, an individual may not be aware
that his/her drinking is causing problems; or may not really think

about the problematic side of their drinking; or may think about the problematic side in an unworried fashion; or they may have been sent by someone.

CONTEMPLATION   Here, an individual acknowledges the link between behaviour and problems; he or she tries to work out what is going wrong; starts to think about their inappropriate use; begins to ask 'Why?' At this stage the client starts to consider altering his or her behaviour, and even to think seriously about change. This stage includes a decision-making evaluation of the pros and cons of both the problem behaviour and the change.

PREPARATION   In this stage, the decision-making is resolved; and a serious commitment to action, and to a change plan to be implemented in the short term, is now formulated. DiClemente and Prochaska suggest that the intention to take action needs to be within the next 30 days for someone to be in the 'preparation' stage. The change plan may include getting specialized help and/or detoxification. At the end of this stage, the person puts the process into action.

ACTION   The client decides to change his/her behaviour and takes steps to do so. S/he implements the proposed action or change: he/she constantly practises new skills which have been learnt to enable change, so as to maintain the new habits or behaviours. If the successful action is sustained for three to six months, the client moves into the maintenance stage.

MAINTENANCE   This stage is the one of trying to integrate the behaviour change into the lifestyle, trying to maintain the chosen direction. It is 'staying stopped'. The temptation gradually decreases; avoiding the behaviour gradually becomes less central to the individual's life.

The latter parts of the action stage and the maintenance stage are the often ignored parts, where the change in drinking habits has occurred. The client has stopped or drastically altered his or her drinking behaviour; the client now has to face up to the difficulties that beset someone once they have changed their behaviour and lifestyle.

TERMINATION OR LAPSE/RELAPSE   The new behaviour has been successfully learnt, and the new coping methods are successfully incorporated into the client's repertoire. For most, however, the next stage is lapse, or relapse, which is particularly common in the first six months, when the person succumbs to the pressures to resume problematic drinking. One of the most interesting developments of the past fifteen years has been the work of Marlatt and Gordon (1985) on relapse prevention, which examines both how to avoid lapses and how to stop lapses becoming relapses (Chapter 5).

These ideas have continued to be developed and debated. A useful book given over entirely to this model was edited by Miller and Heather (1998), and contains many chapters about both the model itself, and the evidence base for it; and Rollnick, Mason and Butler's excellent book demonstrates how many of these ideas are applicable across all health care areas. I see Prochaska and DiClemente's model as clear and commonsensical, and there are a number of points which need to be made about it in relation to our counselling practice.

Change has various stages, and *the change process is a cycle.* People usually make more than one attempt before succeeding. Much evidence suggests that many problem drinkers (70–80 per cent) will go through these stages a number of times in the course of their drinking career. This reiterates the point that relapse is common when dealing with these and other problems.

These two ideas are central and obvious, both to the cycle of change model and to our understanding of the counselling process. Unfortunately, however, this is lost on many who are still committed to the medical, or disease, model, which until recently was the dominant one in the UK (Chapters 1 and 2), and which still holds to an all-or-nothing approach.

If a client comes with a problem of depression, few counsellors would insist on counselling the client only if they arrived happy, and had been happy over the period since the last session. And yet this is exactly what many counsellors do with those who have drinking problems: they say they will see them only if they no longer show the very problem which has brought them to the agency in the first place. Yet if they could control their alcohol intake, they would not need help. Not being able to do this is not a sign of 'lack of motivation' – it is a sign of the problem for which they want our help.

Effective help takes into account the cycle of change. People may present for help at any of these stages:

- they may be sent (pre-contemplation);
- they may be worried and already thinking about their drinking, and therefore open to information and to a careful clarification of the pros and cons of various options (contemplation);

- they may come having decided to take action but are unsure what action to take: open to confirmation that action is correct, with some guided brainstorming about which action is best (preparation);
- they may be in the process of taking, or have already taken, action but be uncertain if they are doing things right, or how to sustain their changes in the short to medium term (action);
- they may have maintained these changes for a bit, but be very unsure as to how to maintain their new behaviour in the long term, and how to incorporate the changes into their lifestyle, or how to change their lifestyle to incorporate their altered drinking practices (maintenance);
- or they may have lapsed and not know how best to get back on to the cycle of change: they may be open to suggestions as to what best to do now (lapse).

The model is not a linear one. Although Figure 3.1 implies that if people relapse, they return to the contemplation stage, in fact people can re-enter the cycle at any point following a lapse. They can return to a pre-contemplative stage by putting up sufficient mental defences to avoid having to face the issues they were facing before relapsing. They can go back into the cycle at the contemplation stage: 'Why did I relapse then? What happened to my determination and strategies?' They can re-enter at the action stage: 'I know what happened, and why. I'm ready to have another go at taking action now, but I need to devise new strategies to enable me to cope with these problematic situations.' Or they can re-enter at the maintenance phase: 'That was a lapse, and I've already stopped drinking. But I can see that the problems I had are likely to arise again when I've been dry for a long period, so we need to work out some new ideas as to how best to cope with these issues.'

Motivation is not seen as a static concept. It is seen as one which will clearly alter as people move from one position to another. For example, those at the pre-contemplative stage do not think that altering their behaviour is a worthwhile task, and hence both their ambivalence about drinking and their motivation to change will be at a low level; those in later stages will be far more ambivalent, and the balance between changing and remaining where they are will be a far more unstable one.

The skills and techniques used at one stage need not be the ones used at another. People at the pre-contemplative stage think less about their problematic behaviour; they spend less time re-evaluating themselves as drinkers; they experience fewer emotional reactions to the negative aspects of drinking; and they do little to shift their attention or their environment away from drinking. To help them, therefore, we need to utilize techniques which increase the time they spend thinking about their alcohol use. We need to get them to re-evaluate themselves as drinkers, to shift their attention away from drinking – all techniques which will be examined in the next chapter.

At the contemplative stage, people are most likely to respond to feedback and education as sources of information about drinking, and they are more likely to feel and think more about themselves in relation to their problem behaviour; they are open to information.

Clients at the preparation and action stages will employ a variety of cognitive strategies such as positive self-talk (telling oneself that stopping is possible); counter-conditioning (teaching oneself to do something else instead of drinking when one feels the need to, for example, relax or be sociable); stimulus control (where one removes from the environment things that seem linked to drinking, which will be different things for different people – it might be the smell of alcohol, or the sight of someone drinking, or the knowledge that alcohol is in the house), as well as behavioural strategies such as self- and social-reinforcement for changes, and the use of the helping relationship for support and understanding.

Clients at the action and maintenance phases will need to emphasize counter-conditioning and stimulus control processes because rewards are less important, and will need to use more behavioural methods such as engaging in alternative behaviours, or altering their environments to remove the cues associated with excessive behaviour.

How all these techniques may be used specifically with clients with alcohol-related problems will be outlined in the next chapter.

The process of counselling and the cycle of change

It is important to stress that a cycle of change model is *not an alternative* to the six-stage model described earlier. The two fit well together.

The six-stage model describes the processes through which our counselling sessions should travel; the model informs us as counsellors as to *the tasks which we have to carry out*. As counsellors we are not in charge of the content of counselling – to a large extent that is determined by the client and what he or she brings to the sessions. We can of course influence this, by the questions we ask and the way we respond to the sorts of things that a client says to us; but the content is primarily up to the client.

The opposite, however, is the case as far as process is concerned. It is our job as counsellors to control the process, to ensure that sessions have a structure, that there is time for us to summarize, for the clients to say what they want to, to discuss action between sessions, and so on. Clients often come to sessions feeling uncertain and chaotic, and it is up to us to provide a framework within which they can feel safe: then they are able to start, or continue, to work on their problems. The model describing the six stages of the process of counselling helps us by providing a framework we can use to give a structure for our clients. 'Content' is the client's responsibility – our job is to be in charge of the 'process'.

The cycle of change on the other hand, describes *the processes through which the client will go* when they change their behaviour. The focus of the Prochaska and DiClemente model is not on the process of the counselling sessions, but on the client's journey.

Finally, Rollnick, Mason and Butler (1999) have taken these ideas and the interchange between the cycle of change and the process of counselling one step further. They have suggested paring all of these ideas down to three central issues: readiness, importance, and confidence. They argue that 'readiness to change' is a central concept underpinning the Prochaska and DiClemente model: depending on the client's readiness to change, they have different needs and should be treated accordingly. And they suggest that

> if a change appears *important* to [a client], and [if the client has] the *confidence* to achieve it, [then the client] will be *more ready* to have a go, and more likely to suceed. When you are sitting in front of [clients], understanding their feelings about these three topics will take you to the heart of the complex forces which surround the topic of behaviour change. (1999: 18)

Rollnick and his colleagues suggest that there are key questions relating to each of these issues. These would frequently be useful for us to go through with our clients. They include:

- under *Importance*: 'Why? – is it worthwhile? why should I? how will I benefit? what will change? at what cost? do I really want to? will it make a difference?'
- under *Confidence*: 'How? what? – can I? how will I do it? how will I cope with x, y, and z? will I succeed if . . . ?'
- under *Readiness*: 'When? – should I do it now? what about other priorities?'

Key points

- Counselling is a process. As counsellors we have the task of facilitating the process. We have to be able to take the overview, see how far we have gone, and organize the sessions so that the counselling is successfully ended.
- The content of sessions is led by the client, although we influence it by our questions and responses to what is said.
- Developing trust is the underpinning of all counselling relationships and counselling stages. Exploring clients' problems is a way of helping them to clarify the issues and to reduce their sense of chaos. Helping clients to gain clarity and a new perspective on previously inexplicable behaviour is insufficient if we do not help them to change or manage that behaviour.
- Clients will often believe there are no alternatives, or that only one possibility is conceivable. A fundamental belief expressed in my counselling is that there are always alternatives. The goal-setting and action stages are concerned with enabling clients to realize this.
- Moving from goals to action involves having a detailed strategy of exactly how the client will put any goal into action. This strategy must involve contingency plans to deal with eventualities that otherwise would negate the overall plan.
- Maintaining the changes involves dealing with different pressures to making the change in the first place. Clients may need to develop new and different skills to deal with these problems. Support from us within the counselling relationship is often crucial during this stage.
- Ending counselling is a necessary but sometimes difficult stage. Ideally, counselling ends when the client realizes he or she has learnt the skills which will enable future problems to be dealt with in the same ways that the difficulties which were initially presented were.
- The range of skills which can be utilized at each stage is large. It is vital to remember the importance of helping clients to change their behaviour. The elements of performance, practise or rehearsal, and homework are tremendously helpful.
- Frequent high-quality supervision is essential. Supervisors should utilize the same process model that is so useful in counselling itself. Effective support and supervision is based on trust. The supervisor needs to explore issues and concerns with a counsellor, rather than imagine that he or she knows what those concerns are. The supervisor needs to help the

counsellor focus on plans, understanding of the problem, feelings for the client, and how these might interact with the work which is being attempted. The supervisor needs to help the counsellor to take action by helping him or her to plan how to implement in a counselling session the strategies and ideas which have emerged during the supervision meeting.

- Prochaska and DiClemente suggest that the client goes through a number of stages: pre-contemplation, contemplation, preparation, action, maintenance, and lapse or relapse.
- The cycle of change is not an alternative to the six-stage model depicting the process of counselling. The two fit well together. One is a model of the process through which our counselling sessions should develop; the other describes the processes through which clients will go when they change their behaviour.
- Another useful way of thinking through the complexities of behaviour change is to work with clients on the relationship between the *importance* of the proposed change to them, their *confidence* in making that change, and their *readiness* to try to achieve that change.

References and further reading

Training packs
Burnard, P. (1996) *Counselling Skills Training*. London: Kogan Page.
Egan, G. (1990) *Exercises in Helping Skills – a Training Manual to Accompany the Skilled Helper*. Belmont, CA: Brooks/Cole.
Inskipp, F. (1986) *Counselling Skills – a Teaching Pack*. Cambridge: National Extension College.
Tolan, J. and Lendrum, S. (1995) *Case Material and Role Play in Counselling Training*. London: Routledge.

General
Banks, N. (1999) *White Counsellors – Black Clients: Theory, Research and Practice*. Aldershot: Ashgate.
Bayne, R., Nicolson, P. and Horton, I. (eds) (1998) *Counselling and Communication Skills for Medical and Health Practitioners*. Leicester: BPS Books.
Dryden, W. and Feltham, C. (1992) *Brief Counselling*. Buckingham: Open University Press.
Egan, G. (1990) *The Skilled Helper*. Belmont, CA: Brooks/Cole.
Hawkins, P. and Shohet, R. (1989) *Supervision in the Helping Professions*. Milton Keynes: Open University Press.
Hough, M. (1998) *Counselling Skills and Theory*. London: Hodder & Stoughton Educational.
Howe, D. (1993) *On Being a Client: Understanding the Process of Counselling and Psychotherapy*. London: Sage.

Jacobs, M. (1998) *The Presenting Past: the Core of Psychodynamic Counselling and Therapy* (2nd edn). Buckingham: Open University Press.

McLeod, M. (1998) *An Introduction to Counselling* (2nd edn). Buckingham: Open University Press.

Murgatroyd, S. (1985) *Counselling and Helping*. London: Methuen.

Palmer, S. and McMahon, G. (eds) (1997) *The Handbook of Counselling, Second Edition*. London: Routledge.

Rollnick, S., Mason, P. and Butler, C. (1999) *Health Behaviour Change: a Guide for Practitioners*. Edinburgh: Churchill Livingstone.

Seden, J. (2000) *Counselling Skills in Social Work Practice*. Buckingham: Open University Press.

Spouse, J. and Redfern, L. (eds) (2000) *Successful Supervision in Health Care Practice: Promoting Professional Development*. London: Blackwell Science.

Stewart, W. (1997) *An A–Z of Counselling Theory and Practice*. London: Nelson Thornes.

Woolfe, R. and Dryden, W. (eds) (1996) *Handbook of Counselling Psychology*. London: Sage.

Alcohol-specific

Alcohol Concern VACTS: Doherty, C., Hoare, I. and Velleman, R. (1991) *Training Volunteer Alcohol Counsellors: Training Guidelines*. London: Alcohol Concern VACTS.

Alcohol Concern VACTS: Doherty, C., Jones, K. and Owen, H. (1992a) *Training Volunteer Alcohol Counsellors: Involving Volunteer Counsellors*. London: Alcohol Concern VACTS.

Alcohol Concern VACTS: Wood-Bevan, M., Doherty, C. and Sainsbury, E. (1992b) *Training Volunteer Alcohol Counsellors: Supervising Volunteer Counsellors*. London: Alcohol Concern VACTS.

DiClemente, C. and Prochaska, J. (1998) 'Towards a comprehensive, transtheoretical model of change: stages of change and addictive behaviours', in W. Miller and N. Heather (eds) (1998) *Treating Addictive Behaviours* (2nd edn). New York: Plenum.

Marlatt, A. and Gordon, J. (eds) (1985) *Relapse Prevention*. New York: Guilford.

Miller, W. and Heather, N. (eds) (1998) *Treating Addictive Behaviours* (2nd edn). New York: Plenum.

Prochaska, J. and DiClemente, C. (1983) 'Transtheoretical therapy: toward a more integrative model of change', *Psychotherapy: Theory, Research and Practice*, 19: 276–88.

Shaikh, Z. with Reading, J. (1999) *Between Two Cultures: Effective Counselling for Asian People with Mental Health and Addiction Problems*. London: Ethnic Alcohol Counselling in Hounslow (EACH).

Shaw, S., Cartwright, A., Spratley, T. and Harwin, J. (1977) *Responding to Drinking Problems*. London: Croom Helm.

Ward, M. (1988) *Helping Problem Drinkers – a Practical Guide for the Caring Professions*. Canterbury: Kent Council on Addictions.

4

Specific Issues concerning Alcohol

There are many specific issues concerned with counselling problem drinkers. This chapter is in two parts. The first covers the specific issues of raising the topic of drinking and identifying problem drinkers; assessing a problem drinker; and dealing with withdrawal. It also discusses some issues around craving and addiction. The second part covers dealing with clients' ambivalence about changing their use of alcohol; giving information; focusing on what clients want to achieve in terms of their alcohol use; helping them to rethink their use of alcohol; and teaching them new skills to deal with difficult situations.

TALKING ABOUT DRINKING

Raising the topic of drinking and identifying problem drinkers

Pip Mason, in her outstanding training manual *Managing Drink* (1989), outlines four problems that arise when counsellors raise the issue of drinking with clients: legitimacy; the client's fear of being judged; the need to contemplate; and the worker's confidence.

Legitimacy
The legitimacy issue relates to the question 'Why raise the issue in the first place?' As counsellors we might ask the question, 'Is his or her drinking any of my business?' This pertains to our role with the client. If we are working in an alcohol advisory centre, then clearly someone's drinking is our business; but if we are working in another agency, the issue is not so clear-cut: a client's drinking is only our business as long as it bears on our role within the agency. Now the fact is that alcohol can have a large influence on almost every aspect of any client's life, as discussed in Chapter 1,

so it always can be seen to be within our role to enquire about alcohol; but this must be done sensitively, explaining to the client why we are asking these questions.

To use some of Mason's examples, if as a health visitor, say, or a doctor our role is to be concerned about health, it is legitimate to ask about alcohol at the same time as asking about smoking, nutrition, and so on; but if our role is, say, that of a social worker who is concerned about a child's positive development or failure to thrive, we can enquire about drinking only in so far as the drinking might affect that child and the standard of care he or she is receiving. If we are seeing someone as a debt counsellor, then it is legitimate to enquire about expenditure on alcohol at the same time as examining other expenditure; whereas questions phrased in terms of health issues or recommended drinking limits might not be legitimate.

The client will also have views about what is and is not our business, and these must usually be respected. Having said that, most clients will not object to questions about their drinking; the vast majority are accepting of such enquiries as long as they can see the link between the drinking and the help they are seeking. It is therefore important to be explicit with the client as to why we are asking the questions we are asking. If we do, the client will be more likely to come with us; if the client is mystified, our questions will serve to increase his or her anxiety, and make it more likely that the client will resist our questioning.

Another issue related to legitimacy is that even if we see that drinking is or could be related to our role with the client, why raise the issue when we know it may lead us into problems? Sometimes the issue cannot be left – if a client arrives at any place offering counselling reeking of booze and with a bottle in his/her pocket, then it is not only legitimate to ask about drinking, it is difficult not to (although some counsellors actually do avoid talking about alcohol in these circumstances!). But if a client comes to a doctor, or a social services office, why should alcohol be raised at all?

Because alcohol problems are so common, alcohol should be on the agenda of all helping agencies: the probability is that a substantial percentage of clients will have alcohol-related difficulties. In all assessments it is worth having the question 'Is there an alcohol-related difficulty here?' in our minds. If we avoid addressing the question, it will probably get in the way of all our other work.

There are some common signs and symptoms which relate to alcohol misuse (Table 4.1), and if a number of these signs point in

Table 4.1 *Common signs and symptoms suggesting an alcohol-related problem*

1   At work
(a) Drinking
- being intoxicated at work
- smelling of drink – generally, or in the mornings, or often after lunch
- bottles found in desk
- drunkenness reported – by the drinker, or colleagues, or supervisor
- drunkenness being associated with arguments, or aggression, or crime

(b) Non-drinking
- absenteeism, especially on Mondays or Fridays
- frequent illnesses or sick leave
- excessive lateness, especially on Monday mornings, or taking long lunch hours or returning late, or being sleepy in the afternoons
- spasmodic or deteriorating work patterns, such as poor time-keeping, poor or deteriorating work performance or low productivity, missed deadlines, making bad decisions, making mistakes due to inattention or poor judgement
- high accident rate, at work or elsewhere
- problems with colleagues
- unreliability, or difficulty in pinning down, or difficulty in settling
- reluctance to accept authority

2   Social
(a) Financial
- debts, or borrowing money from colleagues
- requests for advances of pay
- shabby clothes
- rent or mortgage arrears
- inexplicable lack of money

(b) Legal
- drink-driving or drunkenness conviction
- other legal problems – shoplifting, assault

(c) Accidents
- road accidents, as driver or pedestrian
- accidents at home, or at work

(d) Family
- marital difficulties, or separation or divorce
- abuse – spouse or child
- family history of alcohol problems
- problems and complaints in spouse, especially anxiety or depression, or in children, especially aggression, anxiety, poor school work, bedwetting

(e) Social
- single male, over 40, heavy smoker
- socially isolated
- loss of usual hobbies or interests

continued overleaf

Table 4.1   (*continued*)

3   **Medical/physical**
   • frequent consultations
   • multiple, vague or inconsistent complaints
   • stomach complaints – gastritis, upset stomach, dyspepsia, diarrhoea, ulcers
   • headaches, blackouts, memory lapses
   • tremor, or sweating
   • flushed or puffy face
   • smell of drink at interview, or use of peppermint, perfume or mouthwash as camouflage
   • inappropriate behaviour in surgery, including truculence, loud speech, violent gestures

4   **Psychological**
   • irritability, or unaccountable moodiness
   • anxiety and shakiness
   • depression
   • impotence, or other sexual problems

the direction of an alcohol-related problem, then we should raise the issue and investigate further.

The fear of being judged

If the first question was 'Why?', the second one must be 'How?', which relates to the client's fear of being judged. As the cycle of change in the previous chapter showed, how we do anything depends on what stage the client has reached. Nevertheless, the best way to raise the issue is always to ask the client about his or her drinking, bearing in mind that one should always do this in a warm, non-judgmental, trust-developing way.

A consultant physician I knew always opened his dealings with 'alcoholics' with a gambit along the lines of 'We both know that all alcoholics are terrible liars, but for once be honest – how much are you currently drinking?' Now this does raise the issue directly, but it also raises an immediate barrier. The lack of trust is not because of anything the client has done or said; it is there simply because of the category in which the doctor placed him or her. It is possible this strategy worked for some people and they gave him information in an honest way; but it shows no respect for the client, and hence must serve to reduce the chances of the client returning.

This was demonstrated graphically in 1962 by Chafetz et al., who showed how altering the way clients with drinking problems were treated on their first encounter had a huge effect on whether or not they returned for future appointments. Initially, clients were generally greeted by people who were rude, judgmental, and uncaring. They trained these people to be courteous, polite, and helpful, raising the percentage of clients returning for their next appointment from 5 per cent to 60 per cent, and of those returning for five appointments from 1 per cent to 45 per cent.

I recommend a different approach to that of the consultant physician, which could be as simple as 'Can you tell me how much you are drinking at the moment?'; or slightly more open, such as 'Have you ever thought that alcohol might be contributing to your current problem(s)/to what is happening in your life at the moment?' Such a strategy will work for all clients other than those in the pre-contemplation stage, who are not allowing themselves even to be aware of any difficulties; asking them directly will probably lead to a defensive denial reaction.

The most important issue to consider in these instances is why clients are at the pre-contemplative stage at all. If they simply have never thought about the issues, they will be open to information about alcohol and its effects. The more likely scenario, however, is that they do recognize at some level that drinking is an issue, but feel sensitive about this, and will be easily threatened by questions. The task, then, is to raise the issue in an unthreatening way that will help the client to begin to contemplate changing.

When people approach agencies for help, they are likely to have ambivalent feelings and expectations concerning both the extent to which they actually *want to give up or reduce* their substance use, and the extent to which they *will be able* to achieve this goal. This ambivalence needs to be recognized and worked with. The best way to do this is on the back of the trusting relationship which we have already built, or are in the process of building. The strategy is to join with the client in discussing alcohol in a non-threatening way.

One good way to do this is to raise the issue in terms of the positives which drinking gives, for example that drinking can be a good way to relax after a hard day, or that drinking during social occasions can be fun. Once we have done this, it will be easier to move on to a discussion of any negatives associated with drinking.

MOTIVATIONAL INTERVIEWING   This fits in with another relatively new development in the alcohol-counselling field – the techniques developed in 1983 by Miller called 'motivational interviewing', which have been further refined since then (Miller and Rollnick, 1991; Rollnick and Miller, 1995).

Traditionally, motivation has been thought of in a black-or-white way: clients are either motivated or not. This is often used in hindsight to explain why intervention was not effective: 'The client wasn't motivated enough to change/to return/stay at the hostel/treatment unit/etc.'

Miller argues that motivation is inexorably linked to ambivalence. Instead of ambivalence being seen as a lack of motivation or resistance to treatment, it should be seen as a realistic appraisal that a major shift in lifestyle – which a serious alteration in drinking habits would mean – must have both positive and negative consequences. The positive ones might include improved health, the negative consequences might include a reduced or altered social contact with the group with which the user has associated, which might be quite large and include spouse, colleagues, and close friends.

Miller states that traditionally clients have not been encouraged to talk to counsellors about their ambivalence because such a discussion was seen as the client revealing his or her lack of motivation to change, or resistance to treatment. Good counselling, however, must enable the client to appraise such pros and cons, and at some stage of their lives to conclude that the answer is neither black nor white.

Miller, then, believes that a precursor to working therapeutically with a client with alcohol problems is to clarify the advantages and disadvantages of continuing, modifying, or curtailing drinking.

The notion of drawing up a balance sheet is not new. Janis and Mann originated the idea in their 1968 work on addictive smoking, getting clients to examine the pluses and minuses associated with each of several ways of resolving their difficulties over smoking. This idea – termed variously a 'decision matrix' or a 'pay-off matrix' – has been utilized in the alcohol field, and in the addiction field generally.

What is important is the recognition that there are both positive and negative aspects of excessive drinking, reduced drinking, and abstinence, and that these can be addressed without recourse to terminology such as 'lack of motivation', 'denial', or 'resistance to treatment'.

The counsellor must accept that ambivalence about change is normal, and work with it from the outset – as opposed to ignoring it until a client 'fails' in treatment, and then using 'lack of willpower' as an explanation.

It is not surprising that clients feel uncertain about their ability to change. Most clients will have attempted to alter their behaviour on many occasions without success before seeking professional help. Moreover, they will share many of the socially agreed stereotypes about 'alcoholics' being unable to stop or cut down, being addicted, lacking in willpower, and so on. The second part of this chapter includes methods of altering such negative expectations. The key point, however, is that approaches that incorporate a motivational interviewing component (such as Motivational Enhancement Therapy within Project MATCH) do seem to work better, and deliver better outcomes, than do most other ways of intervening.

The need to take time to contemplate

This is the third issue raised by Mason. By this she means that if someone is just starting to contemplate, they need time to weigh the advantages and disadvantages of changing; the last thing they need is to be pushed too rapidly into a discussion of how to change. For example, if a client has just started to think about his or her drinking, what is needed is a counsellor who listens, empathizes, and draws out the pros and cons of any change using the balance sheet. Above all, the client does not need a counsellor who moves too quickly into asking him or her to take any decisions, or even into suggesting that one set of ideas is superior to another.

On the other hand, if a client has been contemplating for some time, has worked through the pros and cons either with us or on his or her own before coming for counselling, and is ready to take a decision and to start acting – or even has already taken the decision and is already starting to act – then simply examining pros and cons in a warm and empathic way will not be enough. The client will probably get quite frustrated at having to go over old ground, and must be allowed to move on to planning action. The client may even need us to take a firm stand as to which decision we think he or she should come to.

This again raises the importance of being able to assess the stage a client has reached. With an 'early contemplator', taking a firm stand could push him or her into taking up an opposite position, as the client feels forced down a road which has not yet been chosen. The client would probably become resistant, irritated, angry, or obstinate. Whereas if we did exactly the same things with a client towards the end of the contemplation stage, when he or she is ready to move, the client would feel reassured, and the decision would be reinforced.

Talking about 'assessing the stage' that someone has reached leads on to clarifying how best to do this. My own approach is quite a simple one. Paper and pencil tests do exist (overviewed in DiClemente and Prochaska, 1998), but there are problems with them, and my own preference is to share with a client the 'stages of change' model, and to ask them where they feel they sit on it. In my experience many clients find the model as useful as most counsellors have, and they are well able to assess whether they are just starting to think about things (and hence need help in working through the pros and cons of change), ready to take action (and hence need help and advice over what to do), or needing help in maintaining behaviour change in the face of temptation.

The worker's confidence

The final issue Mason addresses is the confidence which the counsellor has. One reason we may not ask about drinking is because we fear we might be correct: the client does have a drinking problem, will reveal all to us, and we will then have to deal with it! We fear that we do not have the skills to deal with it, so the question is best left unasked.

Again, because counselling problem drinkers is like counselling anyone else, if the client tells us about their alcohol problem, we simply explore, help to set goals, empower into action, help to maintain that action, and end our counselling – in exactly the same way we would if we were dealing with any other counselling problem. There are also other techniques which are especially relevant, which the second part of this chapter, and all the following chapter, cover.

Assessing the problem drinker

Having raised the question, or having a client who raises it for us, we are faced with the issue of assessing to what extent the drinking is a problem, or is contributing to other problems. We should examine a number of factors:

- the client's alcohol use;
- the drinking behaviour;
- the effects of the use of alcohol;
- the client's thinking concerning the alcohol use (expectations, values, definition of the problem, understanding its cause);
- the context (family, employment, social) within which the client has been drinking.

Every day, keep track of what you drink, and put down where, why and with whom you drank.

Day	Morning units	Afternoon units	Evening units	Total units
Sun				
Mon				
Tues				
Wed				
Thu				
Fri				
Sat				

Total units this week   _____
Target total units   _____

Figure 4.1   *A drinking diary*

Information regarding some of these will emerge during our counselling sessions, but for an accurate assessment of other factors, some useful techniques have been developed.

Assessing clients' use

The first thing to do is look at the drinking. Surprisingly, a lot of people, with and without drinking problems, have only a vague and general knowledge of how much they drink, so simply asking the client may not result in accurate information. There are a number of ways that produce more accurate details. The best of these works by getting the client to monitor his or her drinking over the following week or two, in a systematic fashion, collecting information about how much is consumed, when, where, and with whom. This activity is known as self-monitoring, and is often described in the alcohol field as a drinking diary (Figure 4.1).

A client will need a diary chart, which can be a photocopy of Figure 4.1, and a list of the quantity of alcohol contained in different drinks (which is obtainable locally from most alcohol advisory centres, or nationally in the UK from Alcohol Concern, or the Health Development Agency, whose addresses are given at the end of this book).

The drinking-diary task is an excellent way of helping us and the client to gain a fuller understanding of the quantity, frequency, and other aspects of a client's drinking. Getting a client to monitor his or her own behaviour serves a number of other functions as well, as outlined in a later section which discusses ways of raising clients' awareness about the environmental determinants of their drinking (p. 80).

It is possible, albeit with less accuracy, to collect this data by a careful questioning of the client about the previous week's activities and drinking. This is best approached as a joint exercise, with the client and counsellor working backwards from 'yesterday', elaborating the client's activities; identifying all possible times alcohol could have been consumed; and clarifying exactly how much and the circumstances in which this was consumed.

This is not an inquisitorial interview – if this is the atmosphere, we have lost the session and probably the client. Good counselling work will only occur in an atmosphere of mutual trust and collaboration. Clients may of course feel defensive about revealing what they drink; and may wish to 'smokescreen' (possibly by arguing that 'everyone knows now that drinking is good for your health'). This particular issue relating to alcohol and health is discussed in Chapter 9, but more generally, it is part of our job as counsellors to create an atmosphere which is conducive to our clients feeling sufficiently undefensive to be open with us. As Rollnick and colleagues say (1999: 113) 'It is a conversation, not an investigation.'

Collecting this information will give us and the client basic data on quantity and frequency of drinking, and on drinking practices – where, with whom, when, and so on. From this we can assess together the extent to which the client is drinking beyond the recommended limits (see p. 8), which in itself may help the client to alter the balance sheet in favour of reducing or stopping. The quantity levels will also indicate the likelihood of the client experiencing withdrawal symptoms if he or she stops drinking too abruptly. If the amounts being consumed are hugely higher than the recommended limits, some counsellors may think that it would be meaningless to raise this issue or make this comparison. I disagree – it is always potentially useful to draw to our clients' attention when they are damaging their health, and the disparity between consumption levels and recommendations can often be a useful way into further discussion and interaction.

A second set of issues relating to clients' use of alcohol is their drinking history, covering the evolution of their drinking, and important changes in the past. There may be, for example, times when clients' drinking increased or decreased substantially, or when they experienced periods of abstinence or control.

Another significant change relates to the experience of altered physiological response to alcohol: for example, some clients report 'reverse tolerance' – instead of being able to drink a lot without getting drunk, suddenly they become drunk on a small amount. Alternatively, they may report withdrawal effects when stopping or cutting down, or the day after drinking, such that they drank to reduce these symptoms.

Effects of alcohol

A number of issues raised in the last paragraph relate to the effects of alcohol. Often these will be asked about in an interview, but other techniques might be used, such as standardized questionnaires like the Michigan Alcohol Screening Test (MAST), or the Severity of Alcohol Dependence Questionnaire (SADQ); interviews with other family members; and physiological measures such as liver function tests, with blood samples being taken to examine the effects of long-term alcohol use, and see if any physical damage has been done. Liver function tests look for raised enzymes in the blood from a damaged liver. Those most commonly performed include GGT (gamma glutamyl transpeptidase) which is the most sensitive and the usual enzyme found to be abnormally high. Other tests of liver function include AST (aspartate aminotransferase; the previous acronym for this was SGOT) and ALT (alanine aminotransferase). GGT could be raised after a significant 'binge' of alcohol and would come back to normal in a matter of days to weeks of abstinence, depending on how much it was raised. Abnormally raised AST and ALT are more indicative of damage to the liver and will take longer to return to normal, if at all, if significant damage has been caused. There may be local differences in which actual tests are included in the 'liver function battery'. In addition there is variability in how sensitive an individual's liver is, so a liver function result which is 'normal' does not mean that large quantities of alcohol have not been consumed, nor is the reverse true.

Another physiological measure is the size of the red blood cells (MCV), usually looked at as part of the same blood test. These cells become larger because alcohol has poisoned the bone marrow which makes these cells. This test will stay abnormal until the bone marrow has a chance to recover and produce normal cells again. The life of a red blood cell is 120 days, so it may take several months for the MCV to return to normality. Blood tests returning to normal can also be used as positive feedback to the client to help them remain abstinent.

Performing liver function tests is not something the average alcohol advisory centre does, but if I suspect there may be physical damage because the drinking has been very heavy and/ or over a long time period, I usually suggest to the client that he or she request from their doctor that one of these tests be performed, or I ask the doctor directly, if there is any contact between us.

Dealing with addiction, withdrawal and craving

When people drink alcohol frequently, their bodies become used to it. This often has two consequences. The first is tolerance, which means the body 'tolerates' alcohol better than it did. Alcohol does not have the same effect as it used to, so a person will need to drink more in order to experience the same effect. The second consequence is withdrawal, which means that if the body does not continue to get the alcohol it has come to expect, the person will experience physical symptoms, which might range from slight discomfort to a major life-threatening epileptic seizure or to delirium tremens.

In what circumstances might we as counsellors be confronted by a client experiencing withdrawal symptoms? Clearly this will only occur when clients are cutting down or stopping their use of alcohol, but whether they experience withdrawal effects at all during stopping, and if so, how serious these effects are, relates to the regularity and quantity of consumption. As a rule of thumb, if clients drink alcohol every day, or most days, and if they consume more than the equivalent of 15 units per day (men) or 10 units per day (women), they are quite likely to experience them. However, because people's physical makeup varies so much, some clients might experience some slight withdrawal effects on stopping after drinking, say, half those quantities, whereas others might drink considerably more and still not experience withdrawal.

Generally, dealing with withdrawal is a medical issue. Although many clients do stop or cut down on their own, others often need medical help to do this, in the shape of withdrawal relief. Stopping drinking is often termed 'drying out' or detoxification (or 'detox'). It used to be the case that this was usually organized in an in-patient hospital setting, so as to effectively control an individual's withdrawal symptoms, but increasingly 'detox' is being dealt with in individuals' own homes, with hospital detox being increasingly rare.

Although dealing with the withdrawal effects is a medical issue, we will often have to deal with them indirectly, by advising clients about problems which might arise, or helping them deal with these problems once they have arisen. They need to know they have to be cautious about simply giving up alcohol if they have been drinking heavily. They will also need to be aware of what the symptoms of withdrawal are, such as shaking, feeling sick, sweating, and mood changes. It may be helpful to point out that these symptoms often mimic the initial problems – of tension, depression, and so on – which may have been the reason why the drinking became problematic in the first place. They will also need to know that some of the effects of withdrawal may take two to three days to fully appear. In addition we need to advise our clients on what to do if withdrawal symptoms do occur. For example, we might suggest to a client that he or she get some short-term medication from his or her doctor to relieve the worst of the withdrawal symptoms. One psychiatrist I know suggests to her clients that, if they cannot get medical help for very 'severe' withdrawal, then drinking alcohol would be safer than persisting with abstinence – especially if they have had a seizure previously or if they are medically unwell. Clearly, advising clients to have a drink when they are trying to stop is something to be done with a great deal of caution and a lot of thought!

It is also useful to advise our clients about ways in which they can help reduce any withdrawal symptoms, other than by taking medication. For example, if clients drink plenty of fluids, eat regularly even if they don't feel like it, and create an environment with as little stress in it as is practical, withdrawal symptoms will be greatly reduced. David Cooper's useful book on detoxification (1994) examines ways of assessing and dealing with many of these issues.

As I outlined in Chapter 1, there are many disagreements and controversies over how we understand alcohol problems. The previous sections have been concerned with the effects of alcohol as a drug: a drug which has strong effects on people's physical makeup, leading to withdrawal symptoms, alterations in liver functioning, changes in blood cells and so on. It is easy to see why many people do see alcohol problems as a physical addiction, where people have become 'hooked' on a drug (alcohol) and where their bodies (and even the cells in their bodies) cry out for the substance and set up such strong cravings that people have to succumb.

This is not the model I adopt in this book. I do of course recognize that there is a physical component to the development and maintenance of alcohol problems (which is why I have included the sections above). But I also believe that the physical component is both far less important, and far less amenable to being intervened with, than is the psychological. This is not to say that people do not experience what we choose to call 'craving'; but this is simply a term we use to describe what people say to us – which is that they feel a need or an urge or a strong desire for something. Calling it 'craving' does not make it any more or less real – it is just a name describing a set of experiences. It is my belief (and my experience backs this up) that working with people at a psychological level, using the techniques outlined in the previous chapter, and in the remainder of this chapter and the next one, enables people both to understand their feelings (including their craving) and their behaviour, and to take action to change them so that they no longer cause them problems.

INTERVENING WITH DRINKING PROBLEMS

Effective Interventions

Some methods of intervention are more evidence-based than others (Miller et al., 1998), and the range of intervention ideas contained in the following pages is based on these, as opposed to other, less evidence-based, approaches. Project MATCH utilized the most evidence-based interventions and demonstrated that these approaches were generally very effective in helping people with alcohol problems. The evidence-based approaches they used were Motivational Enhancement Therapy (MET) and Cognitive Behaviour Therapy (CBT), and they also included 12-Step Facilitation (TSF) as it was so dominant an approach within the USA.

Project MATCH showed that people who were helped using any of these methods improved markedly. They

> demonstrated major improvements in drinking, as well as in other areas of functioning such as depression, use of illict drugs, and liver enzyme status. Overall, MATCH clients were abstaining over 85% of the days throughout the year following treatment and alcohol consumption decreased fivefold. Even those not successful in maintaining abstinence who continued to drink experienced a substantial reduction in alcohol consumption. (Mattson, 1998: 166)

The ideas underpinning MET have already been outlined in Chapter 3 and in the first part of this chapter and are implicit in much of what follows in this chapter and in Chapter 5. The majority of the specific interventions and techniques in the remainder of this chapter and in Chapter 5 are primarily underpinned by a clear CBT approach.

Clients' expectations and ambivalence

Clients usually arrive at a helping agency with ambivalent feelings and expectations concerning two things. The first is the extent to which *they want to give up or reduce their drinking*. This ambivalence needs to be recognized and addressed at the outset, and a number of techniques have been offered in the first part of this chapter and in Chapter 3 to enable us to raise these issues in a way that will serve to increase a client's motivation and reduce their ambivalence.

Most clients also will arrive with ambivalent feelings as to *whether or not they can* change their behaviour: most will have attempted to reduce or stop drinking before coming to see a counsellor, and will not have totally succeeded, otherwise they would have no need to come.

The following pages provide an outline of methods that have been found helpful in enabling clients with alcohol problems to reduce or stop drinking.

Giving information

One important method – and indeed an important responsibility – is to give clients accurate information about alcohol so they can make their own decisions. The need to ensure that clients have the necessary information arises because many people start using alcohol excessively because they do not know how much is too much. They also do not know about the different strengths of different beverages, for instance, or the different effects of alcohol on men and on women.

Accordingly, one aspect of health promotional work in recent years has been to provide people with the necessary information to make informed decisions about how much, when, where, and with whom, to drink alcohol. A crucial point underlying the pro-vision of this type of information is that it is linked to behaviour change. It is interactive information, appealing to the general population, which has as its aim the raising of people's feelings of self-efficacy.

Giving advice and information in the first session seems to be an effective way of helping. One study conducted in the 1970s (Orford and Edwards, 1977) discovered that simply giving clients in a single session a small amount of information and advice on how to cut down or give up – and why they should do this – led to as much change in behaviour as did a full range of alcoholism treatment services; this was especially the case with problem drinkers who were less severely physiologically dependent. It has subsequently been shown that doctors giving similar simple advice can also be effective in enabling problem drinkers to reduce or stop.

A third line of evidence links these two: the provision to those with developing problems of written information and advice concerning alcohol. This method was first attempted in the USA with the publication in 1976 of Miller and Munoz's *How to Control Your Drinking* and subsequently evaluated in a number of studies. This work has been continued in the UK by Heather et al. (1987), who advertised in the national and local press, inviting readers who thought they were drinking too much to write for free advice. Those who responded were given a structured self-help manual, which gave information about alcohol and its effects, and advised readers on how to decide whether or not they had an alcohol problem. It then went on to show them how to analyse their reasons for drinking, the cues associated with their heavy drinking, and suitable and relevant alternatives which might fulfil the same needs as the drinking. This self-help manual was subsequently issued as a self-help book in the UK (Robertson and Heather's *So You Want to Cut Down Your Drinking?*, now revised as *Let's Drink to Your Health!* by Heather and Robertson, 1996). All these methods revolve around enabling individuals to better assess and understand their behaviour.

Information-giving has also become so important because many clients only attend a single session, so getting information across in the first session is essential.

In addition, information can help clients by alerting them to the dangers of high-risk situations (Chapter 5).

Focusing on goals

Behavioural methods of intervention have for many years argued for the need to set manageable, realistic, and achievable goals (the SMART goals discussed in the previous chapter), against which clients and counsellors can measure progress. This is equally important in the alcohol field. By the time someone has sought help, he or she will usually have developed problems in a number of areas of life functioning, as well as having difficulty in controlling the use of alcohol.

The goals set must address some or all of these issues. Yet for many clients, the enormity of the range and number of problems will seem insurmountable. A good strategy, as discussed in Chapter 3, is to help the client to set intermediate goals which are, and seem to the client to be, achievable in the short term. Furthermore, being short-term, these goals will be realized relatively quickly, which will lead to a range of rewards for the client, such as a sense of greater satisfaction and increased self-efficacy, or tangible rewards, such as greater financial stability or better employment or family relationships. Achieved goals and rewarded action will in turn sustain and reinforce the client's sense of commitment to change, and keep the balance on the reduction-of-use side of the balance sheet.

Another area discussed in the preceding chapter is that the goals should be the client's, not ours. If the goals are not the client's, he or she will not achieve them. For example, in examining goals concerning future drinking, a number of studies have randomly assigned problem drinkers to either a goal of abstinence or one of controlled drinking. Such studies show that very few of the 'abstinence' clients managed to abstain, although most severely moderated their drinking. The reason was that most of the individuals assigned to 'abstinence' rejected the goal from the outset. When problem drinkers are allowed a choice about the kind of help they receive – as opposed to being given a standard treatment regime which is the same for all clients – the success of intervention tends to improve.

How to agree drinking goals

There are a host of still controversial issues relating to whether or not controlled drinking is a viable intervention aim (Chapter 9). The orientation of this book is that such goals are legitimate ones to aim towards, if any individual client wishes to. Controlled drinking may be a legitimate aim, even if its only merit is ultimately to convince the client that it was an unrealistic one.

As with everything else, if we want to know what a client is aiming for, it is best to ask him/her. However, it is difficult to help clients towards their goals if we do not believe that what they are trying to do is sensible. If we are committed to an abstinence framework, or, alternatively, to a belief that all clients should control their drinking as opposed to abstaining, then it may be difficult for us to support a client who is aiming in the opposite direction.

Controlled drinking is more difficult than abstaining. Abstaining is simple – you just do not drink any alcohol at all. Controlled drinking, however, is open to negotiation and change, to clients miscalculating (deliberately or accidentally) how much they have drunk. Furthermore, alcohol has a disinhibiting effect, which may mean that a client who feels totally certain that he or she will keep to the prearranged limit before starting to drink may experience a change of mind once the first pint (or three) has been drunk.

Helping clients to control their drinking means they have to be committed to doing a variety of things:

- carefully monitoring their drinking, to be clear they are keeping to the prearranged limits;
- being absolutely clear about what those limits are;

- utilizing strategies that mean it is far more difficult to renegotiate these limits, such as going to a pub much later, taking only a limited amount of money, telling drinking companions what the limit is, and asking them to help by not offering alcohol once the limit has been reached.

It also means we and the client must have agreed exactly what we both mean by controlled drinking. As outlined in Chapter 1, controlled drinking is not a euphemism for normal or social drinking: it means a person has to be aware, possibly for the rest of their lives, of exactly how much they are drinking, when, where and with whom. *Controlled drinking is very difficult*. An example of a controlled drinking programme, and the necessary skills which a client needs to acquire, are discussed later in this chapter.

Finally, what do we do if we think the client is aiming for the wrong goal? Continuing with the philosophy that it is always best to be open and honest with clients, we should tell them we are happy to back them up in their choice of goal, but also that we personally think they have chosen incorrectly, and *why we think this*.

Although the evidence is that people succeed better if they are pursuing the goal of their choice, there is also evidence that some people are more successful at pursuing a controlled drinking goal than others (Table 4.2).

Individuals with the characteristics outlined in Table 4.2 appear to be at greater risk of failing to keep to one or other of the drinking goals. However, these research results tell us about the *relative* chances of success, as opposed to some absolute certainty of success or failure. Hence, it is not the case that a young, socially stable client aiming for controlled drinking will succeed, or that an older, more dependent drinker with little stability will not – only that their chances are altered by these factors. There will always be clients whose outcome is different to the one predicted on the basis of the research evidence.

In summary, my answer is to tell the client why I am concerned about his or her goal, but to also tell the client there are individuals who do better than the research would predict, and that he or she might be one of those, and that whatever is aimed for, he or she can rely on my support and help.

Helping clients to believe they can change

A number of methods have been devised for clients who want to give up or cut down on their use, but who believe they cannot, to

Table 4.2   *Indicators for and against controlled drinking*

Those more likely to succeed with controlled drinking	Those more likely to succeed with total abstinence
Those choosing controlled drinking	Those choosing abstinence
Those who are younger	Those who are older
Those in employment	Those who have no social stability in terms of stable relationships, employment, and accommodation
Those with a family around them	Those with less support from family and friends
Those with a shorter history of misuse	Those with a longer history of heavy drinking
Those with less physical, mental, or social harm caused by their drinking	Those suffering from physical damage such as liver disease, or mental damage such as memory loss
Those with lower consumption before coming for help	Those who have tried and failed to control their drinking
Those showing no signs of physical dependence	Those who are more severely dependent in terms of having more physiological indices, such as more severe withdrawal, high (or reversed) tolerance, etc.

Sources: Heather and Robertson, 1983; Ward, 1988

help them change this belief. These include raising their awareness of the environmental forces that push them towards drinking, and then using more active techniques to help them to rethink what they can do.

Raising awareness

This involves getting the client to collect good-quality information about what he or she is doing. Many clients come with only a very general knowledge concerning their drinking, which is heavily biased by their negative belief in themselves – they selectively perceive negative events about themselves, and examples of their loss of control. A first step in challenging this is to get the clients to monitor their behaviour in a systematic fashion, collecting information about how much is consumed and when, where, and with whom.

When this process of self-monitoring was described above, I was using it as a way of assessing the quantity, frequency, and so on of a client's drinking, and indeed it is useful as a method of collecting such information.

Getting a client to monitor his or her own behaviour has, however, a number of other functions as well. It helps the client to begin to take control: instead of having a counsellor assess him or her, the client collects his or her own data. Next, it enables a client to get a better knowledge of how much drink he or she is actually consuming – something which he or she usually does not know. It also makes a client aware of the circumstances in which the activity occurs – what actually triggers a drinking bout – and it may serve to clarify the restraining forces which keep the behaviour in check at some points or with some people. It also enables precise goals to be set on the basis of a more detailed knowledge of the present behaviour; and it provides a baseline against which subsequent progress may be compared.

In addition, self-monitoring requires a client to do something in between the sessions, which is a useful thing as it aids the continuation of any positive changes, and reinforces the idea of the process of change being the client's responsibility as well as the counsellor's. It is often the case that simply getting a client to focus on his or her alcohol use is an effective therapeutic technique, with clients reporting a reduction in their intake when they realize its extent.

Other awareness techniques were described by Wallace (1985), and include:

- 'practising the opposite', which focuses awareness on habitual ways of approaching and responding to typical situations;
- 'following the drunk through', which involves the client imagining vividly the entire drinking episode, concentrating on the more delayed negative consequences as well as the initial positive ones;
- 'talking to yourself', in which the client, in a group setting, has a conversation with him or herself, alternating between two chairs, one person being the sober and one the drunk self, in order to 'sharpen and clarify the inner conflict commonly encountered'.

Restructuring the way clients think about their behaviour
These techniques for raising awareness provide a basis upon which we can help a client to rethink his or her behaviour. The question is: how best to do this?

Although some practitioners argue that direct confrontation is the most effective method, my experience is that it has to be used very carefully indeed. Our task as counsellors is to join with the client to facilitate him or her to think about the behaviour, take action to change it, and maintain a stable lifestyle that does not involve excessive drinking.

Direct confrontation, used other than in a warm and friendly way, and on the back of a positive relationship, is unlikely to work. In fact, it is likely to increase anxiety. This in turn might precipitate some sort of avoidance response – the client might leave counselling, or start to deny the extent or the degree of problems associated with the drinking, which would increase the client's resistance to change. Increased anxiety might also increase the chances of the client returning to excessive drinking.

Another approach is to use indirect confrontation, focusing on the inconsistencies in what the client reports. For example, a client might define him or herself as someone who cannot stop drinking, but tell us about a time when he or she had stopped or controlled his or her drinking. This allows us to respond by asking, 'What was different in your life then?' or, 'How were you able to do that at that time?'

Another indirect confrontation might arise if the client tells us that stopping drinking is impossible, but then reports having come to our counselling session that day without having drunk. If we juxtapose these two messages – 'You say that you can't stop, and yet you have stopped today' – the client may recognize that there are inconsistencies between what is said and what is done. We may then be able to help the client to see that the thinking which leads to these inconsistencies serves to block them from attempting to change.

In one study Oei and Jackson (1982) set out to discover how far a client's irrational beliefs affected their ability to change. They examined four groups of clients: a 'traditional, supportive group', a group where clients learnt social skills (Chapter 6); a group where clients' irrational beliefs and attitudes were challenged indirectly; and a fourth group which combined social skills and the challenging of irrational beliefs.

Although their findings are marred by methodological problems in the study, they found that the latter three groups were significantly superior to the 'traditional, supportive group' control group; and that the last, the combined group, fared best of all.

Other strategies that clients can use to restructure their thoughts include consciousness-raising and self-re-evaluation. What all these techniques have in common is their attempt to get people to think introspectively; to increase their awareness of their behaviour and motivation; to think about themselves in relation to their behaviour; and to question and re-evaluate this behaviour in the light of who they want to be and feel they can become.

Teaching new skills to deal with old problems, and strategies to overcome anticipated problems

Once the client has moved some way through the process of examining the feasibility of the treatment goal and the need for a change in lifestyle, the whole question of implementing desired behaviour change comes to the fore. (Rollnick, 1985)

A major cornerstone of the approach suggested in this book is that getting clients to *do* something – and then to practise doing it until it is second nature – is a more effective and longer-lasting method of helping them to change their behaviour and attitudes than is simply talking about change.

The rationale for concentrating on doing things is simple: if clients have been dealing with a negative situation for many years by drinking, they will lack the skills – or the ability to utilize the skills – to successfully negotiate the future for any extended period of time without drinking. What is needed is to work with individuals to enable them to identify and practise new strategies and skills, so that the alcohol is not required.

Researchers have examined two sorts of skills. The first consists of avoidance strategies, teaching individuals how to recognize problem situations and not to get involved with them; the second involves problem-solving strategies, which teach individuals how to cope with the problem situation once they are in it. Avoidance skills are particularly useful in attempting to prevent relapse and they will be discussed in detail in the next chapter, on relapse management. The remainder of this chapter concentrates on problem-solving skills.

Teaching the skills of controlled drinking

Many problem drinkers have attempted to control their intake in the past and have failed, but a number of studies have shown that controlled drinking can be a legitimate goal, especially as so many clients aim for this anyway. Most studies show, however, that success is dependent on the skills of controlled drinking being taught effectively.

Teaching controlled drinking means analysing the times, places, and cues responsible for the drinking going out of control, and teaching a range of alternative strategies, behaviours, and skills for dealing with these cues. The most well known study of controlled drinking is that conducted by Mark and Linda Sobell (1978). They were working at the time in a hospital in California, where all clients with alcohol problems underwent a traditional in-patient alcoholism treatment programme similar to the one described in Chapter 2 as a style of intervention in the medical/ AA model. In their study, clients were assigned to one of two intervention groups: one group working towards controlled drinking, and the other towards abstinence. Both groups had controls, who had no extra treatment.

Clients in both groups participated in 17 intensive sessions. The content was similar for both groups, except that the controlled-drinking group had sessions orientated towards learning how to control, whereas the other group was learning how to abstain. The controlled-drinking group's sessions included learning about appropriate drinking, problem-solving, assertiveness training, education, coping responses, and watching videotapes of the members' drunken behaviour.

The results showed that at 6, 12, 18, and 24 months both intervention groups were functioning at better levels than the control groups as measured by their drinking outcome; and the intervention group orientated towards controlled drinking had fewer drunken days and fewer days in hospital or jail, more days of controlled drinking and more days abstinent, than did the intervention group orientated towards abstinence. Although these results generated considerable controversy (outlined, for example, in Heather and Robertson, 1983, 1997), similar findings have been shown in many other studies. The point to be made here, however, is not related to the particular results which the Sobells achieved. Instead it relates to the *methods* by which they achieved them: the learning of skills concerning appropriate and safe drinking.

For many clients who have used alcohol in an uncontrolled fashion over an extended period, learning how to drink in a controlled way means relearning, or learning for the first time, basic skills which make it easier to drink less. Many of these seem like helpful tips rather than skills, but what makes them skills is that they need to be learnt and practised. For example, the tip to have something to eat before going out drinking needs to be practised to such an extent that a client will never drink unless he or she has a full stomach.

Some of the skills a client aiming for controlled drinking might use are outlined in Table 4.3.

A brief example of a controlled drinking programme arranged with one of my clients is shown in Table 4.4. The drinking limits and other strategies in the programme were those of John (my client), not mine. They were also set in conjunction with John learning other problem-solving skills, such as how to cope with his anxiety and his depression, two sets of negative emotional states

Table 4.3   *Controlled drinking skills*

Before drinking
- Eat something first.
- Go out later.
- Take less money.
- Don't drink in places where you have previously drunk heavily.
- Take alcohol-free drinks with you to parties, friends' houses, etc.

While drinking
- Drink a long soft drink first.
- Drink halves rather than pints; singles, not doubles; ordinary rather than strong beers or lagers.
- Drink more diluted drinks – spirits with mixers rather than neat, shandy rather than all-beer, half-and-half of alcohol-free and ordinary beer or lager.
- Drink low or no-alcohol beers and wines.
- Drink in sips rather than gulps.
- Put the glass down between sips.
- Don't stand at the bar – sit down elsewhere.
- Drink at the pace of the slowest drinker in your group.
- Alternate between non-alcoholic and alcoholic drinks.
- Time yourself, for example only drink one unit every 30 minutes.
- Avoid crisps and peanuts, etc. – they make you thirsty.
- Avoid rounds, but if they are unavoidable, don't buy yourself one on your round.
- Practise refusing drinks.
- Do something active while drinking – play pool, cards, darts, etc.
- Go home when you have reached your limit.

Sources: Mason, 1989; Ward, 1988

we had identified as triggers for John's drinking. Clearly, the preferred drinks, their costs, and other items can be altered to suit different clients, and the costs will certainly change over the years!

Teaching general problem-solving skills

In 1978 Chaney et al. wrote about the treatment package they had devised to help problem drinkers deal with situations which had been dangerous in the past.

Forty in-patient 'alcoholics' undergoing the conventional hospital treatment regime were divided into three groups: skills-training, discussion, and a no-additional-treatment control group. In the skills-training group, clients were presented with a problem situation, such as 'a row with my spouse', 'getting fired', 'looking foolish in front of my friends', and were then trained to use a problem-solving strategy to deal with it.

The counsellor first selected a non-drinking response, discussed it with the group, and then modelled it. Each group member then

Table 4.4   *A controlled drinking programme*

General issues

Set an overall limit:
- No more than 20 units drunk over the week
- Two days clear of alcohol each week
- No more than four units on any day
- No drinking during the day (e.g. lunchtime), Mon–Fri inclusive
- Possibly (after six months) allow one 'binge' of an agreed maximum (say six units) once a month

Detailed issues
- Alcohol-free days are Monday and Thursday, unless altered by prior arrangement with counsellor or with 'significant other', e.g. spouse
- Problematic drinking was related to spirits, so any drinking confined to beer (pub) or wine (if beer not available, e.g. visiting friends)
- Only drink at the pub after an evening meal

Strategic issues
- Preferred drink is beer
- Preferred place of drinking is the pub
- Cost of preferred beer is £X.xx per pint (to be filled in)

Strategy
- Take no more than twice £X.xx (the exact cost of two pints), plus the cost of two soft drinks, with you to the pub
- First drink at the pub always to be alcohol-free or very low alcohol
- After two units, always have a non-alcoholic drink as a spacer
- Request the publican not to advance you credit
- Ask friends not to lend you money
- Ask friends not to buy you drinks

had to choose their own way of coping with the problem, rehearse this in front of the group, and receive feedback from the group members.

At the end of each exercise, the methods and strategies used were summarized by a group member. There were eight 1.5 hour sessions, and all role play was conducted in the group sessions – there was no real-life practise. When they were followed up one year later, the group members had experienced shorter and less severe relapses than those in the other two groups.

There is a large amount of other research relating to the issue of skills (summarized in Velleman, 1991), but in brief, all the research backs up the finding described above: helping clients to acquire and practise relevant skills as opposed to discussing the issues is of paramount importance.

In one study, clients were assisted in finding jobs, accommodation, and friends, as well as being helped to purchase a telephone and television (this approach has been termed the 'Community Reinforcement Approach', and is summarized in Meyers and Smith, 1995). Those who were taught the skills of interviewing and job-finding, marital and family interaction, how to fill spare time, and how to develop new friendships, had far better success rates than did the control groups.

Another study reported an intervention programme in which clients generated a hierarchy of situations which might trigger excessive drinking, ranging from those that were almost certain to trigger a relapse, to very mild triggers. Each client was then exposed to a range of situations which had been identified by that client as such a trigger, with each successive situation more threatening than the previous one. In each instance the client did not drink; instead he (the clients were all males) performed some alternative behaviour. Some of these behaviours were suggested by the client, some by the counsellor, with the only rules being that the client could not avoid the situation, and each alternative had to be practised. These clients had very positive outcomes, which were maintained over follow-ups of up to nine months.

What this research highlights again is the importance of our clients learning and practising alternative ways of coping with the triggers which normally push them into drinking. Clients who can engage in alternative ways of behaving and who can adopt a positive style of coping appear to do well in the long term.

The implications of such research are that the skills that clients with alcohol problems need are similar to those needed by any other client. We should attempt to teach clients a general coping and problem-solving strategy, which they can then use in specific situations. This is far more useful than merely teaching specific coping responses to individual problems.

D'Zurilla and Goldfried (1971) isolated six general processes of problem-solving: mental set, problem definition, generation of potential solutions, decision-making, verification, and feedback.

Mental set includes individuals' overall approach to problem-solving. A healthy mental set would be one in which problems are seen as a normal feature of everyday life requiring a flexible approach to enable solutions to be found.

Unfortunately, some people believe in TINA (There Is No Alternative), acting as if there is only one possible way of reacting to a problem, rather than realizing there is always a range of solutions and reactions. Others create highly pressurized belief systems which propel them into inescapable situations. An essential first step in problem-solving skills is to learn to understand that problems can affect anyone, and that the skills to overcome problems can be learnt and achieved by anyone.

This counter-productive mental set can lead to a number of flaws which pervade the thinking of people with alcohol problems – or any of a range of emotional and behavioural problems. Examples of these include:

- over-generalization – where, for example, the taking of one drink is seen as signifying total loss of control;
- catastrophization – where one bad event or decision signifies that everything about the person is lacking, and nothing will ever be able to help;
- jumping to conclusions – where one of a range of possible explanations is selected, which shows oneself in a bad light or leads to negative consequences.

Another problem is that of 'shoulds'. The counselling approach of Rational-Emotive Therapy (RET) suggests that some problem drinkers are so heavily directed towards the fulfilment of 'shoulds' about the world that they can only escape such pressure by heavy drinking.

What links all these ideas of 'mental set' is the clients' lack of detachment: their inability to see clearly beyond the immediate confines of the problem so that the range of solutions is apparent.

Problem definition relates to the previous stage, in that many people see their problems in global terms rather than in precise ones. It is only when the problem is delineated in precise terms that the boundaries are clear, and potential solutions become apparent.

Generation of potential solutions involves the brainstorming of solutions – the opening up of a range of possibilities of new responses which might not previously have been considered (Chapter 3).

Decision-making involves the selection from the brainstorming of a small number of solutions which might be feasible and achievable; and from that, one to try out (Chapter 3).

Verification is testing out the chosen solution – by talking it through with others, trying it out in imagination, role-playing, or attempting it in real life.

Feedback means assessing with the help of others the effectiveness of the preferred strategy, and re-evaluating the usefulness of the chosen solution.

These six processes through which people solve problems are similar to the processes of counselling examined in Chapter 3.

This is not surprising, as in some ways counselling people with problems involves enabling them to learn how to solve problems for themselves.

Conclusion

This part of the chapter has concentrated on enabling clients to learn new or alternative approaches to dealing with both the drinking and the difficulties which accompany drinking.

Yet once someone with a long-standing alcohol problem begins to deal with it, a host of new situations and troubles – some completely new, and others the person has not had to deal with for many years – will start to emerge. Effective counselling needs to anticipate and deal with these challenges as well. The way to respond is to use the same range of problem-solving skills described above. Yet there are, for example, particular difficulties in dealing with relapse, which is considered in detail in Chapter 5.

Case study – Harry

In my first session with Harry we talked about his drinking. While I started by giving him the space to talk about his most pressing concerns, which in his case was his grief, it was clear in the way that drinking kept creeping into the conversation that this was an issue which needed airing sooner rather than later. I therefore raised the issue directly, saying: 'When you first contacted me, you told me a bit about your current difficulties with drinking; could you tell me a little more?'

I followed this up by asking Harry to try to list for me all the things that drinking gave him. With help, prompting, and support from me, he revealed a whole catalogue of reasons for drinking, including that it gave him something to do and a place to go where he was known and greeted with friendliness; it enabled him to cope with his grief at the death of his wife; and heavy drinking was a way of life for him stretching back over many years.

I was able to follow this line of investigation by asking him why, if it gave him so much, he wanted to cut down or stop. People had been telling him he was drinking too much, was a drunk, an alcoholic, and that he had to stop. His reaction had been defensive, and had centred around disobeying these instructions. By asking him to convince me that such a functional behaviour pattern as his drinking obviously was, also had a problematic side, I was passing to him the responsibility for the identification that it was a problem.

Harry was then able to tell me of the range of problems associated with drinking, including financial; family – his daughters were upset with him returning home intoxicated; social – he felt that he was beginning to be seen as an 'old soak' in his pub, and in the community; and personal – he felt very guilty over his drinking, knowing his wife would have disapproved of his 'weakness'.

I introduced the idea of monitoring drinking, and got Harry to agree to carry with him and fill out a drinking diary between our sessions. This revealed both the extent of his drinking (he was consuming roughly 30 units per day, the equivalent of a bottle of spirits), and the importance of the pub as a social milieu. This then provided a focus for our counselling. Two key short-term goals were to reduce his high alcohol intake, and to develop alternative ways of providing social contact.

We agreed that Harry would contact his doctor to arrange for short-term medication to deal with the withdrawal effects we could expect at that level of drinking. In examining Harry's goals, he decided he wanted to become abstinent from alcohol, and to develop a wider social network which did not revolve around drinking. I felt this was an appropriate goal, given Harry's age, level of drinking, and the period over which he had been a heavy drinker; although I would have agreed with whatever goal he had come up with, even though I would have expressed my doubts if I had thought it to be an inadvisable decision: client choice is the most important consideration.

Harry's level of awareness about his drinking was already high, and the drinking diary further increased it. What he lacked were alternative ways of behaving, and the skills to carry these out. We brainstormed a number of ideas as to how he could redevelop a non-drinking-orientated social life, such as inviting friends round for a meal, having old friends come to stay, joining a rambling group (he was a keen walker), and accepting invitations to visit others.

We then worked through the problematic points of each suggestion, clarifying solutions to any difficulties, and delineating situations where there was increased risk of Harry returning to drinking. During the time between sessions, Harry put into practice the various ideas. He gradually became more skilled at seeing at-risk situations, at avoiding them, and at utilizing his new-found abilities to deal with rather than drink away difficulties.

Key points

- Four problems commonly arise that hinder counsellors from raising the issue of drinking with clients: legitimacy; the client's fear of being judged; the need to take time to contemplate; and the counsellor's confidence.

- Motivational interviewing is a technique that accepts that ambivalence about changing behaviour is normal. We need to work with this ambivalence from the outset, as opposed to ignoring it until a client 'fails', whereupon explanations couched in terms of 'lack of willpower', or 'lack of motivation' are used.
- In assessing a client's alcohol problems we should examine a number of factors: the client's alcohol use (quantity, frequency); the drinking behaviour (where, when, with whom); the effects of the use of alcohol; the client's thinking concerning the alcohol use (expectations, values, definition of the problem, understanding of its cause); and the context (family, employment, social) within which the client has been drinking.
- In assessing clients' use and behaviour, the best method is to get them to monitor their drinking over the following week or two, in a systematic fashion, collecting information about how much is consumed, when, where, and with whom. This is known as keeping a drinking diary.
- Although counselling clients with drinking problems requires the same skills and processes as counselling for any other problem, there also are techniques which are especially relevant to counselling problem drinkers.
- One important method is to give clients information and advice as to how to cut down or give up.
- There are a number of techniques which help clients to become more aware of their drinking and what pushes them to drink; self-monitoring is especially useful.
- Controlled drinking goals are legitimate to aim towards if the client wishes to. However, controlled drinking is more difficult than abstaining.
- Although the evidence is that people succeed better if they are pursuing the goal of their choice, there is also evidence that some people are more successful at pursuing a controlled drinking goal than others.
- To help clients to develop their own abilities to solve the problems in their lives, it is of paramount importance that clients acquire and practise relevant skills, as opposed to merely discussing the issues with us. Our clients must learn and practise alternative ways of coping with the triggers which normally push them into drinking. Those clients who can engage in alternative ways of behaving, and who can adopt a positive style of coping with problems, appear to do well in the long term.

References and further reading

Chafetz, M., Blane, H., Abram, H. et al. (1962) 'Establishing treatment relations with alcoholics', *Journal of Nervous and Mental Disorders*, 134: 395–409.

Chaney, E., O'Leary, M. and Marlatt, G. (1978) 'Skill training with alcoholics', *Journal of Consulting and Clinical Psychology*, 38: 1092–104.

Colclough, B. (1994) *The Effective Way to Stop Drinking*. London: Penguin.

Cooper, D. (1994) *Alcohol Home Detoxification and Assessment*. Edinburgh: Radcliffe Medical Press.

Davidson, R., Rollnick, S. and MacEwan, I. (eds) (1991) *Counselling Problem Drinkers*. London: Routledge.

DiClemente, C. and Prochaska, J. (1998) 'Towards a comprehensive, transtheoretical model of change: stages of change and addictive behaviours', in W. Miller and N. Heather (eds), *Treating Addictive Behaviours* (2nd edn). New York: Plenum.

D'Zurilla, T. and Goldfried, M. (1971) 'Problem solving and behaviour modification', *Journal of Abnormal Psychology*, 78: 107–26.

Edwards, G., Marshall, E. and Cook, C. (1997) *The Treatment of Drinking Problems: a Guide for the Helping Professions* (3rd edn). Cambridge: Cambridge University Press.

Heather, N. and Robertson, I. (1983) *Controlled Drinking* (2nd edn). London: Methuen.

Heather, N. and Robertson, I. (1996) *Let's Drink to Your Health! A Self-help Guide to Sensible Drinking* (2nd edn). Leicester: BPS Books.

Heather, N. and Robertson, I. (1997) *Problem Drinking: the New Approach* (3rd edn). Oxford: Oxford University Press.

Heather, N., Robertson, I., MacPherson, B. et al. (1987) 'The effectiveness of a controlled-drinking self-help manual: one year follow-up results', *British Journal of Clinical Psychology*, 26: 279–87.

Janis, I. and Mann, L. (1968) 'A conflict theory approach to attitude change and decision making', in A. Greenwald, T. Brock and T. Ostrom (eds), *Psychological Foundations of Attitudes*. New York: Academic Press.

Mason, P. (1989) *Managing Drink*. Birmingham: Aquarius.

Mason, P. and Norris, H. (eds) (1990) *Personal Skills Training for Problem Drinkers: a Counsellors' Guide*. Birmingham: Aquarius.

Mattson, M. (1998) 'Finding the right approach', in W. Miller and N. Heather (eds), *Treating Addictive Behaviours* (2nd edn). New York: Plenum.

Meyers, R. and Smith, J. (1995) *Clinical Guide to Alcohol Treatment: The Community Reinforcement Approach*. New York: Guilford.

Miller, W. (1983) 'Motivational interviewing with problem drinkers', *Behavioural Psychotherapy*, 11: 147–72.

Miller, W. and Heather, N. (eds) (1998) *Treating Addictive Behaviours* (2nd edn). New York: Plenum.

Miller, W. and Munoz, R. (1976) *How to Control Your Drinking*. Englewood Cliffs, NJ: Prentice-Hall.

Miller, W. and Rollnick, S. (1991) *Motivational Interviewing: Preparing People to Change Addictive Behaviour*. London and New York: Guilford.

Miller, W., Andrews, N., Wilbourne, P. and Bennett, M. (1998) 'A wealth of alternatives: effective treatments for alcohol problems', in W. Miller and N. Heather (eds), *Treating Addictive Behaviours* (2nd edn). New York: Plenum.

Oei, T. and Jackson, P. (1982) 'Long-term effects of group and individual social skills training with alcoholics', *Addictive Behaviours*, 5: 129–36.

Orford, J. and Edwards, G. (1977) *Alcoholism: a Comparison of Treatment and Advice, with a Study of the Influence of Marriage*. Oxford: Oxford University Press.

Robertson, I. and Heather, N. (1985) *So You Want to Cut Down Your Drinking?* Edinburgh: Scottish Health Education Group.

Rollnick, S. (1985) 'The value of a cognitive-behavioural approach to the treatment of problem drinkers', in N. Heather, I. Robertson and P. Davies (eds), *The Misuse of Alcohol*. London: Croom Helm.

Rollnick, S. and Miller, W. (1995) 'What is motivational interviewing?', *Behavioural and Cognitive Psychotherapy*, 23: 325–34.

Rollnick, S., Mason, P. and Butler, C. (1999) *Health Behaviour Change: a Guide for Practitioners*. Edinburgh: Churchill Livingstone.

Shaikh, Z. with Reading, J. (1999) *Between Two Cultures: Effective Counselling for Asian People with Mental Health and Addiction Problems*. London: Ethnic Alcohol Counselling in Hounslow (EACH).

Sobell, M. and Sobell, L. (1978) *Behavioural Treatment of Alcohol Problems. Individualized Therapy and Controlled Drinking*. New York: Plenum.

Velleman, R. (1991) 'Alcohol and drug problems', in W. Dryden and R. Rentoul (eds), *Clinical Problems: a Cognitive-Behavioural Approach*. London: Routledge.

Wallace, J. (1985) 'Behavioural modification methods as adjuncts to psychotherapy', in S. Zimberg, J. Wallace and S. Blume (eds), *Practical Approaches to Alcoholism Psychotherapy* (2nd edn). New York: Plenum.

Ward, M. (1988) *Helping Problem Drinkers – a Practical Guide for the Caring Professions*. Canterbury: Kent Council on Addictions.

5

Preventing and Dealing with Relapse

T here are two types of relapse: the type that occurs very quickly, during the early parts of our intervention; and the type that occurs some way down the pathway of change. The first type relates to clients who have tried to move, or who have been pushed, into the action phase too soon, before they have sufficiently dealt with the ambivalence and contemplation issues. Someone who relapses very quickly is telling us, and him or herself, that there is still work to be done in dealing with motivation and ambivalence.

This chapter is mainly concerned with the second type of relapse, which is very different. Here we have clients who have really dealt with their ambivalence, who feel ready to take action, but who do not manage to carry out their intentions. Why is this? It is this question that I will try to answer, drawing heavily on the research conducted by Marlatt and Gordon (1985). This chapter examines the relatively new area of 'relapse management', looking at some of the techniques which have been developed both to prevent relapse occurring, and to manage it if it does occur.

Why has it taken so long?

Although it has been realized for many years that people who were trying to control their drinking (and other behaviour, such as eating, smoking, drug-taking, and gambling) frequently relapsed and recommenced their problematic behaviour, it is only in the past few years that theory and techniques have been developed which have made it possible to do something about this. One of the major factors responsible for delaying the development of a set of techniques to deal with relapse has been the way in which relapse has been thought of.

People used to believe, and many still do, that if we recognize that relapse is likely, and if we discuss this with clients, we are somehow giving the client permission to relapse. There is an element of truth in this: part of the success of counselling lies in our ability to create a situation in which a client can feel hopeful about succeeding. If we started our counselling by telling the client that there was a very good chance he or she would fail, we could see why many people might think this was a bad idea, and would think instead that we should say nothing at all, simply hoping that relapse will not happen. Yet this is not what relapse management is about – no one suggests we should do as outlined above.

People also used to feel – and again, many still do – that getting a client to deal with his or her drink problem is a test of motivation, and that a client can only help him or herself if he or she really wants to. In this scenario, a relapse implies that the client is not yet sufficiently motivated to change successfully.

The problem, then, is that relapse is common, and we need to take measures to reduce the chances of it happening – but without doing things that make it more likely.

As with all the other problems discussed in this book, the solution lies in how we raise and deal with the issues surrounding relapse. If people relapse, it is for reasons. If people do not relapse, it is because they have learnt the skills that enable them to traverse the risky situations that tempt others back into problematic behaviour.

The task is not about giving clients permission to fail; indeed, our task is to do exactly the opposite – to empower and enthuse, and to provide confidence and hope. But it *is* our task to enable clients to think ahead, to anticipate likely problems, to plan out possible solutions to those problems (which might be avoidance strategies, or might be skills which reduce the impact of the difficulties), and to practise those skills and strategies such that their chances of falling foul of some risky situation are greatly reduced.

It is my contention that the best way to help clients to deal with relapse is not to try to hide from them that the temptation to relapse is likely, but to give them the confidence that they will know how to deal with these issues when they arise.

Anticipating problems and their solutions

It is important to get over to our clients once we start to work with them on reducing or stopping their drinking that, whatever happens, they must return to tell us about it. Their task is not to succeed in leading a sober, unproblematic life the first time they make an attempt; the task is to try, and to report back on what takes place.

We are clear that for most clients there will be a great deal of ambivalence about changing. We accept this as normal and expected. The frame of mind we are trying to get our clients into is one in which they are experimenting to see what will work. We have no magic answers, and neither do the clients.

We as counsellors, and the client with the problem, are trying to understand why this client has developed this problem, and what can be done about it. What matters is not the short-term goal of abstinence or control; it is the long-term aim of the client being problem-free in the weeks, months, and years to come, to the extent that any of us are 'problem-free'. The client must try things, possibly fail, and try again. With our help and support he or she will win through. An approach which suggests that a client must abstain, that ambivalence is a sign of a lack of motivation, and that relapse is proof of lack of motivation, will only serve to alienate our clients.

I often discuss relapse relatively soon with clients. First I have them brainstorm with me what they and others (spouse, parents, children, friends, me, others) could do to stop them relapsing in the future. A useful technique is to ask the clients to think of a time when they successfully exerted control, and to examine why that occurred; then to think of a time when they lapsed, and again to examine why that occurred.

Clients often find this exercise difficult. Many will say the relapse 'just happened'. This is not true, and we should not let clients get away with this. This does not mean we accuse them of dishonesty. Clients tell us what is available to be told, and the area of relapse is replete with upset, failure, disappointment – it is no wonder they want to skate over it as quickly as possible. But clients must be helped to see that relapse is not something which 'just happens', but is an endpoint in a chain of decisions and events that may have started some time before the actual relapse. This can be seen easily in the corresponding problem of dieting, where people often plan out their relapses long in advance: it is common for people to say in the autumn that they are dieting for Christmas, the implication being they know they are going to relapse at that time.

It is at this point that I usually introduce the split between preventing a lapse occurring, and dealing with it once it has occurred. I do this by likening the problem drinker trying to regain control over their behaviour to someone walking along the edge of a cliff. People who do not have problems with their drinking walk quite a distance from the edge; although they *could* fall over, they are less likely to. Clients, by virtue of the fact that they *have* a problem, are walking along a path which is very close to the edge of the cliff. What can we do? I suggest two things.

On the one hand, if we put railings along the edge of the cliff, they are far less likely to fall over the edge (this prevents them from lapsing); on the other hand, if we give them a parachute, then if they do fall over, they will be able to land safely and not fall to their deaths on the rocks below (this deals with a lapse if it occurs).

The task of relapse management is to discover why relapse occurs, and to develop strategies which can act as 'railings', and as a 'parachute'.

Continuing the metaphor, it is also vital that we and the client are in agreement on the nature of the cliff. Relapse must be understood in relation to the goals which we and the client have jointly worked out – if the client is working towards controlling his or her drinking, then going to the pub and drinking an agreed amount is not a relapse.

Why does relapse occur?

There are many reasons why relapse occurs, but instead of listing all of them, I am going to offer an examination of the process of relapse, based on the idea that the most effective way of inter-vening is to change the process.

A great deal of work on developing relapse management has been carried out by Marlatt and Gordon (1985), who see relapse as comprising two stages:

- the processes which occur before the first drink is taken – the triggering of a resumption of drinking or other problematic behaviour;
- the processes which occur after that first drink is taken – the continued excessive use.

This division between the two stages has important ramifications for how we can intervene during counselling. Marlatt believes that the two stages are triggered by separate processes, and each has to be dealt with separately in order for us to help effectively. The significance of Marlatt's work is that not only has he provided a theoretical explanation for relapse, but he has also provided a method of attempting to prevent it. He believes that clients must be prepared for relapse, and taught how to deal with potential relapse situations as part of their counselling. This teaching has two parts: recognizing and dealing with at-risk situations (the 'railings') and dealing with a lapse situation so that it does not turn into a full-blown relapse (the 'parachute').

The triggering of the resumption of drinking

Marlatt argues that there are five steps which generally lead to the first drink:

1   An apparently irrelevant decision, leading to . . .
2   a high-risk situation, leading to . . .
3   a no-coping response, leading to . . .
4   a feeling of helplessness and low self-control, leading to . . .
5   a positive expectancy that alcohol will make the problem drinker feel better, leading to . . .

the initial drink

The first step is the 'apparently irrelevant decision'. Clients will often tell us of little things they did which seemed at the time to be totally harmless, but which in retrospect started the ball rolling towards the high-risk situation. Examples might include, 'Getting off the bus at a different bus stop, which just happened to mean I walked past the pub'; 'Accepting an invitation to the leaving do, which meant everyone else was drinking'; and, 'Feeling I was ready to invite some good friends round for a meal, and not realizing they would bring a bottle.'

These and other seemingly irrelevant decisions put people in at-risk situations: suddenly everyone else is drinking and having a good time; or the client passes the pub and smells the old familiar smells; or has the dinner party, and finds an opened bottle of wine left over.

People are going to have to face up to all these at-risk situations (and more), and they are all ones which can be coped with. But clients need to be prepared for them, and have strategies up their sleeves. If they are not prepared or have no campaign to put into action, the next stage of having no usable coping response is reached.

This leads straight on to a feeling of helplessness, low self-control, a *déjà-vu* feeling in which clients feel they have been here before, and are powerless to stop. Coupled with this is the belief and the expectation that drinking alcohol will relieve this awful feeling, even though it will only be short term – 'But what the hell . . .', and the first drink is drunk.

Lapse becoming relapse

Marlatt's second stage of relapse, where people continue drinking once they have started, has four steps:

1   Stress, because the problem drinker has broken the 'no-drink' rule, leading to . . .
2   self-blame, attributing it to 'internal weakness', leading to . . .
3   drinking to reduce the stress, guilt, and self-disgust, leading to . . .
4   the positive effects of the alcohol reinforcing continued drinking.

Marlatt sees the transformation from lapse to relapse as being caused or precipitated by something he terms the 'abstinence violation effect'. The disease model is very strong, and the belief that one must abstain at all costs is well integrated into our culture. After a vow to abstain – whether from alcohol or chocolate biscuits – a slip or lapse is seen as a major failure. Common sense decrees that someone would say, 'It is only one biscuit or one drink', but in fact most people seem to react in a way where one slip is seen to have ruined months of dieting or abstaining to the extent that a person eating one biscuit or having one drink feels he or she might as well eat the whole packet, or finish the bottle.

Marlatt believes this is caused by the client's sense of personal failure or hopelessness; they see their lack of success in keeping to their plans as a sign that there is something fundamentally lacking *in them*. This leads to even greater levels of negative feelings, and further drinking is entered into as a way of relieving such feelings. The short-term success of this further drinking prolongs the bout, until the negative consequences of the drinking start to overtake the positive ones.

Another reason why the first drink leads to total relapse concerns the disease model of alcoholism. Research studies have shown that whether or not clients relapse after a first drink is significantly related to the beliefs they hold. The disease model says one drink will lead to loss of control over drinking, and therefore to relapse. The research shows that the more people believe this, the more likely they are to do so.

It is important to underline the fact that this belief is untrue. If we take two people with the same level of dependency on alcohol, one who believes that a single drink will cause a relapse, the other who does not believe this, the first client will be much more likely to relapse than the second. *The reason people relapse after one drink is not because they have an uncontrollable urge: it is because they expect they will relapse.*

If Marlatt's two-stage analysis of relapse is to be useful, it must not only help us and the client to understand why relapse occurs, but enable us to take action to prevent it.

Preventing relapse before the first drink

A central feature of the relapse management approach is that the possibility of relapse is not hidden from clients, but is openly discussed so that clients have the maximum opportunity to prepare for potential relapse-inducing situations. Mason (1989) uses the analogy of a fire drill, which does not increase the risk of fire occurring, but is instead a realistic attempt at minimizing the damage if one does occur.

The work needed to examine relapse can be done well during individual counselling, but there are good reasons as well for conducting relapse management in a group setting. Brainstorming, developing lists of apparently irrelevant decisions, high-risk situations, and so on, often work even better if there are a number of participants (Chapter 6).

Recognizing apparently irrelevant decisions

This step is concerned with enabling clients to recognize how they get into high-risk situations. It is best done by having individuals and groups brainstorm real and hypothetical high-risk situations. The pathways which led (or could lead) the individual into each of these situations are then described in detail. The aim is to follow each of these paths backwards until the decision which started the person on the road to the high-risk situation is reached.

The technique is the same one used when preparing for job interviews, where one tries to second-guess what questions might be asked. One cannot guess every question, of course, but the more prepared one is to answer the widest range of questions, the more confident one feels, and the less likely one is to be thrown by an odd, unexpected question. If every question is unexpected, one is far more likely to be thrown off balance. Similarly, the more confident clients are that they can handle most situations, the less likely they are to be thrown by a new situation.

Clients also need to be able to locate the apparently irrelevant decision after the event, once they are in an at-risk situation. They must be able to backtrack, and clarify what the early-warning cues were which they missed, so they can learn from each new experience. 'How have I got myself into this mess? What were the early-warning messages? Why didn't I see them? What would I need to do differently to ensure I don't get into this sort of mess in the future?'

The vital thing is to enable clients to take avoidance actions so they do not get into high-risk situations in the first place. The task is to identify the pathways into at-risk situations so clients can recognize them and avoid them. It is also to explore the skills needed to successfully avoid these situations: how to refuse invitations, or not succumb to the social pressure to drink, are two examples of the skills needed.

Monitoring and analysing high-risk situations

Avoidance actions will not always work. Often clients will find themselves in a high-risk situation, and will then have to deal with it. Each identified high-risk situation will already have been analysed in the counselling sessions to extract the decisions which led to it, so appropriate avoidance actions could be delineated which the client could take to ensure he or she does not get into the situation if it arises. Each one should be analysed again so that the specific alternative skills needed if the client cannot avoid the situation can be delineated and practised.

Of course, what count as high-risk situations will vary greatly. For some clients, the high-risk situation will be something which catches them unawares or unprepared; but for other clients, life in general is high risk. Their difficulty is with coping – not with a party where there is lots of alcohol, but with the dull, boring, bleak grind of living. For others, the high-risk situation is waking up feeling depressed and moody; for others it concerns conflict with other people; and for yet others it is dealing with the fact that being sober is not as much fun as being intoxicated – the expected positives have not outweighed the realized negatives.

Each of these situations is manageable, and coping strategies can be developed to deal with all of them – but the situations must be recognized in order for them to be dealt with.

Teaching coping responses

The analysis of high-risk situations should have clarified which coping responses are needed. The client, in conjunction with the counsellor, now needs to decide which of these responses are already available, and which need to be acquired. Skills needed will probably include anxiety-management skills, social skills, and assertion training (Chapter 6). Other skills will relate to dealing with the difficulties within relationships and family life (Chapter 10). Yet other skills are those of filling time, dealing with negative emotional states, dealing with frustrations, and asking important others (e.g. family and friends) for support and help.

Marlatt suggests that all of these skills are more likely to generalize and become long-lasting if they are practised in real-life situations. Clients should place themselves in increasingly difficult situations, and practise these new coping strategies until they are confident they can use the techniques once they are no longer in counselling.

We should remember that coping does not only mean dealing with the particular issues inherent within any single high-risk situation. Often, clients find the expected advantages of sobriety do not outweigh the disadvantages, and return to drinking as a deliberate act. Clients need to gain the skills of coping with the daily grind of living in a world that is sometimes dull and boring, and sometimes unfair.

This raises the issue of long-term as opposed to short-term coping; the issue of maintaining change as opposed to simply taking action, which was discussed in Chapter 3. In the short term, clients can generate many alternative actions which they might utilize instead of drinking. But it may be that more fundamental changes are necessary if clients are to deal successfully with their problems in the long term. For example, they may need to consider changing their job if it is one which puts them into too many high-risk situations, or dealing with difficulties in their relationship if these repeatedly lead to risky situations.

Amongst the valuable ideas in relapse prevention work (along with reviewing decisions, awareness of high-risk situations and developing coping responses or avoiding them, self-monitoring for warning signs and developing a crisis drill) is the concept of lifestyle balance. In the time before a relapse there is often an imbalance between the 'shoulds' and 'wants', with the client being weighed down with obligations and inner resentment. It is worth working with these feelings with clients and enabling them to recognize these as important warning signs.

Dealing with helplessness

People feel helpless because they do not believe in themselves sufficiently to believe they can change things. Sometimes this is a realistic view: no individual can hope to singlehandedly change the system. But often this view has arisen because people have experienced many situations where their actions have led to negative outcomes, and where they have felt they had no control.

Part of our task is to enable clients to feel more hopeful, more in control, that they have the ability to change things, both directly in their lives (their drinking habits, for example) and in their wider experience.

So, we have a situation where clients feel powerless and hopeless; and we know that it is important they feel more in control. The answer is to work with the clients to encourage them to do things which lead to them experiencing control: we need to help our clients to create situations which lead to positive experiences. If they act in situations and find there are positive outcomes, they will develop a more positive sense of self-worth.

It is our job to explore with the client particular tasks or activities which might lead to positive outcomes. These outcomes do not have to be material, or even gained from other people, although of course they can be. A positive outcome might be the client feeling good about him or herself because of something done, or some past set of achievements re-evaluated.

For example, if a client has successfully abstained or controlled his or her drinking for a longer period than previously managed, we might ask the client to reflect on this in the session, and get the client to hear him or herself recount a success story. We might then suggest that the client tell someone else – a friend or a relation – and get positive feedback from this other person as well.

Clearly it is essential that the other person can be depended upon to give a positive response. This is not a trivial issue. Many clients will be surrounded either by other drinkers who might not provide positive feedback relating to reducing drinking, or by family and friends who have lost faith in the client's ability to take positive action. A more typical reaction here might be, 'I've seen all this before: you'll be back on the booze tomorrow', which can become a self-fulfilling prophecy.

Reducing clients' positive expectancies about the effects of alcohol
The final link in this chain is the expectation that drinking alcohol will lead to positive results, at least in the short term. This is a difficult view to shift because it is largely true: drinking alcohol in the short term will blur the negative edges, and may also make a client feel more light-headed, more talkative or more charming.

The best way of tackling this is via alcohol education. Many clients are surprisingly ignorant about all sorts of facts related to alcohol. Increasingly, alcohol agencies are offering courses for clients, covering such issues as the more negative short-term effects (violence, slurring, stupid behaviour), and the negative long-term effects of alcohol on health, sexuality, social relationships, and so on.

Dealing with a lapse situation

All the steps outlined by Marlatt that occur after the first drink, which translate a lapse into a relapse, revolve around the abstinence violation effect. Breaking abstinence leads to full relapse for a few key reasons. First, there is a strong all-or-nothing element to people's decision to control their behaviour – the eating of a packet of biscuits after eating only one, as mentioned previously. Second, there are a number of processes which work to make continued drinking more likely once someone has started. And third, the disease model tells people that taking one drink will inexorably lead to loss of control. As we have seen, if people believe this, it will happen. Three suggestions to break the link between lapse and relapse can be made, arising from this analysis.

Changing clients' understanding

The link needs to be broken between having a lapse and entering into a full-scale relapse. To break this link effectively, we need to provide clients with information, and possibly act more as a persuader than we might commonly do as a counsellor. This does not mean we tell clients what to do, or try to force them to change their views. Such tactics are doomed to failure: it is very difficult to make people do or believe things they do not wish to do or believe.

But we can help to change our clients' understanding in a variety of ways. If clients are committed to the disease model, we need to try to alter the 'one drink equals one drunk' idea. We can inform clients of the evidence that this is untrue, and that it is only thinking it will happen which causes it to.

If we do attempt to change this view, we will need to be careful we do not inadvertently suggest that it is perfectly all right for the client to take that one drink. Clients need to be clear that because there is no *necessary* link between one drink and all the rest does not mean it is safe to take that first one. If they have resolved not to drink at all, they may still feel upset at their failure, and this perceived failure might then lead on to a full relapse; they need to know why controlled drinking is both very difficult and not at all like 'normal' drinking (Chapter 4). Furthermore, there are many problems associated with a 'just one will be OK' belief. Counsellors often see a stepwise pattern of escalation following that first drink (described by Chris Johnstone, a colleague in Bristol, as the 'whirlpool effect') which starts with an idea that 'I can handle it'. In the related field of giving up smoking, it is common practice to advise people to avoid having 'just one' because of the accepted high risk of escalation. Many people do report with smoking that 'just one cigarette' leaves them with significant craving the next day, increasing the chances (but not making it inevitable) that a single lapse will turn into a full-blown relapse.

So – clients need to be helped not to make slips: not to take that first drink (if they are aiming for abstinence). But they must also be persuaded not to view a slip as a personal failure that will inevitably lead to a full relapse. They need to realize they are attempting to learn a new set of skills – and, as with any new skill, mistakes will occur. No one would expect to learn the skill of riding a bicycle without one or two tumbles, or the skills of typing without one or two errors, so why expect to learn the skills of living without alcohol without these slips? Some of the advice Marlatt gives his clients concerning the prevention of a slip becoming a relapse is to:

> look on the slip as a learning experience. What were the elements of the high-risk situation which led to the slip? What coping response could you have used to get around the situation? . . . Look upon the slip as a single, independent event, something which can be avoided in the future by the use of an appropriate coping response. (Marlatt and Gordon, 1985)

We also need to explore with clients how for them a relapse may escalate out of control. Chris Johnstone uses the term 'relapse amplifier' to describe anything that makes continued drinking more likely once someone has started. For example, the disinhibiting effect of alcohol can make it easier (but not inevitable) for drinking to escalate. Another is the 'All or nothing thinking' I have explored above: 'in for a penny, in for a pound' or 'once I've started I might as well continue'. Negative feelings and emotions such as guilt, shame, and failure also enable lapses and relapses to escalate out of control. As I say above, one of the values of Marlatt's work is that it helps us to break out of the blaming and shaming that can follow relapse, and reframe the experience as an opportunity for learning.

The practicalities of dealing with a lapse

Hopefully, clients no longer expect a lapse to lead to a relapse. They may see that taking a drink is not the end of the world. But they still need to know what to do if they lapse. What skills do they need to enable them to stop after one drink (or a small number of drinks)?

There are a number of skills, which can be divided into things the client can say to him or herself, and things the client can do.

VERBAL SKILLS   These include saying a variety of things to themselves and others:

- There is no necessary connection between lapse and relapse.
- Turning a lapse into a relapse is catastrophizing the world.
- What I do is under my own control.

The client should also:

- rehearse the advantages of remaining on their pre-planned path of not returning to excessive drinking;
- calculate the money saved by not drinking;
- think about the improved relationships with family, friends and colleagues.

BEHAVIOUR   Verbal strategies are useful, but often desert people's minds just when they are needed. Many clients report that before the lapse occurred they knew exactly what to say to stop themselves, but when they did take that first drink, they felt panic-stricken, and could think of nothing to do except to carry on drinking. There are a number of useful behavioural strategies to prevent a slip turning into a full-scale relapse.

Marlatt suggests that clients are given a set of 'reminder cards', which are sealed but which clients carry around with them and which are only opened after a slip has occurred. These cards rehearse the self-talk discussed above. Another strategy is for the client to tell as many people as possible about his or her aspirations about drinking, and to ask people to say some of the things discussed above if they see him or her start to drink. These people could also be asked to help by not offering the client alcohol.

PROGRAMMED LAPSE   If one accepts that, even with the strategies outlined in previous sections, a lapse is likely, it is important to prepare for it. The ideas above are all useful in preparing clients to deal with a lapse, but as with any skill, thinking about how to do something is not the same as actually doing it. People do not commonly learn to ride a bike by rehearsing what they would do, and by carrying around a set of instructions concerning what to do when they first try riding. Instead they practise the skills. So one idea for stopping a lapse becoming a relapse is to provide a 'controlled' or 'programmed lapse'. This involves the client 'lapsing' under the supervision of the counsellor, with the client rehearsing some of the 'controlling' strategies outlined above.

This is an idea which worries many counsellors. There is a concern that if I accompany a client into a drinking situation and encourage him or her to practise the controlling strategies outlined above, I might be both speeding up the relapse process, and 'giving permission' for the drinking to recur.

My own view on this is different. Clearly such an activity must be undertaken with both care and clarity on the part of both myself as counsellor, and my client. But if we accept that part of what we are doing is enabling our clients to learn new skills, we also need to accept some responsibility for helping clients to practise them. I would not think very much of a driving instructor who only outlined driving skills in off-road situations, and then refused to accompany the learner driver on to the road! As with the learner driver, before I go into this type of situation I need to be as convinced as possible that my client has understood and learnt the basic steps that we have gone through, and that the context of the programmed lapse is as conducive to a successful outcome as possible. So my client and I need to choose the timing and the environment, and plan our programmed lapse, very carefully (I would not want the learner driver's first experience to be attempting to drive around Hyde Park Corner in London).

However, as with all the other ideas in this book, counsellors should not undertake things that they are not comfortable with, and they should not do things which countermand the policies under which the agency with which they work operates. All the ideas in this book will be useful for some counsellors; few will feel completely appropriate for everyone.

Dealing with feelings about relapse

Even with all the hard work that will have gone into attempting to guard against a lapse, and trying to stop a lapse turning into a relapse, they will sometimes occur. How should we deal with them?

The most important thing of all is to ensure that the client returns, so the issue can be discussed and dealt with. But what should we do when the client does return? I have already said that clients need to alter their view of relapse as a failure to seeing it as an opportunity for learning. This is easier said than done, partly because we as counsellors may also be experiencing the same sense of failure and guilt ('If I was a better counsellor, this wouldn't have happened'); both may feel depressed, or annoyed, or simply hopeless. If we disclose our negative feelings to the client, this may lead to him or her feeling even more responsible and guilty, and generally negative.

There is no simple answer as to what to do about these feelings. As counsellors, we must be open with the client about our feelings, but only in so far as these will be helpful. The counselling session is for the benefit of the client, not ourselves, and we must ensure we do not offload our negative feelings on to him or her. That is something which we do in supervision, where we should be helped to work through all our negative feelings. It is our job to do the same things for the client: that is a central part of our relationship with him or her; it is our task to ensure that the client leaves feeling hopeful again, and that these issues have been acknowledged and dealt with.

If the relapsed client returns, what we do must depend on how he or she presents the situation. If it is presented as something from which the client has learnt, we must go through with him or her exactly what has been understood. Why did it occur? What can the client do to stop the situation occurring again? What can he or she do if this proves impossible and the situation does recur? One thing that may have been learnt as a result of a relapse is that the goal of controlling drinking may be inappropriate for this client at this time.

If the client presents the relapse as a catastrophe, we must go through the issues outlined earlier, trying to show them that it can, and indeed must, be viewed positively; that it is only a catastrophe if the client makes it one. Once this is achieved, we must then go through the lessons learnt above.

If the client comes having relapsed and making light of it, then it is our job to help them to see it is potentially a serious issue, and that relapses can lead him or her right back into the abyss of serious alcohol problems.

Conclusion

The framework developed by Marlatt represents a huge step forward in developing our understanding of relapse, and what to do about it. The model of relapse management described con-centrates on three elements which will have become familiar by now: understanding the reasons for a client's behaviour; under-standing the central role that a client's expectations and beliefs play in determining his or her behaviour; and enabling a client to learn new, and utilize already learnt, skills.

For the client, the important issues are to learn to recognize early warning signs; monitor high-risk situations; develop coping strategies for these situations so that they do not turn into lapses; and set up coping mechanisms so that lapses do not turn into relapses. Perhaps the most fundamental of all the elements for the client is the shifting of emphasis from thinking of relapse as a failure, to seeing it as a learning experience, with the concomitant need to clarify what has been learnt as a result of the lapse. This does not mean that we should encourage our clients to relapse (although we may decide to undertake a programmed lapse, as outlined above); but it does mean that we should expect and accept relapses, and enable our clients to learn from them.

Case study – Harry

Harry benefited from the relapse management approach. When he first came to see me, he had tried lots of different approaches – Alcoholics Anonymous, private treatment agencies – and had relapsed frequently. We discussed this at an early stage, and made two decisions: first, that we needed to work through possible relapse-inducing situations, and second, that if a relapse occurred, it was vital that he return so we could discuss and learn from it.

Harry made many apparently irrelevant decisions. For example, one strategy to improve his social life that we decided upon was to invite friends round for a meal, and Harry did not think through what he would do when people arrived bearing a bottle of wine.

Harry became better at recognizing when situations were likely to become risky, and he developed many skills at avoiding these at-risk situations. For example, he arranged with the friends who came for a meal that they would take away with them any leftover alcohol, so he would not need to keep any in the house. I got him to rehearse out loud in the sessions how well he was doing – and indeed, he remained abstinent for a longer period than he had ever done in the previous thirty years.

However, Harry did start to drink again. He came to me in distress because he had drunk two pints. We discussed the detail of what had happened. As a result of this lapse, he decided he wanted to try controlled drinking. I told him of my view that the evidence suggested this would not be a good idea; but he still wished to try, and so I supported him in this.

He then had a major relapse. He telephoned me rather than coming to an appointment, slurring his words. I pressed him to come anyway, but he refused, feeling he had let both himself and me down. I made another appointment, and he did not come. I wrote twice more and telephoned once. In all, I had three conversations with an intoxicated and terribly ashamed Harry. Finally, he returned after two months. I saw this as a great success – I had managed to convince him that we could still work together in spite of his 'failure', as he saw it.

I worked to enable Harry to reframe the situation, to see the relapse as a tremendous learning experience. We reverted to an abstinence goal, and to continuing to work on analysing at-risk situations, developing better coping skills, and raising confidence and self-esteem. We also worked on dealing with any future lapses in such a way that they did not turn into relapses. After two months, we moved to fortnightly sessions, then to monthly, and two three-monthly follow-ups.

Key points

- Intervening to prevent relapse has been attempted only in recent years. Before that, counsellors felt that even discussing relapse gave people permission to return to drinking; they also used to think that relapse was a sign of lack of motivation.
- As relapse is so common, we need to discuss it in counselling sessions, with a view to helping clients to find ways of avoiding it. This needs to be done in a way which enables clients to understand that avoiding relapse is possible, if they do the right things.
- Clients need to know that, even if they do relapse, we still want them to return to discuss the situation with us.
- Marlatt separates relapse into two components: the processes which occur before the first drink, and those which lead to a lapse becoming a full-scale relapse.
- These two components include nine stages which lead to relapse. There are things which can be done to prevent relapse at each stage.
- Some clients will nevertheless relapse. Both they and we will have negative feelings about this. Our negative feelings must be dealt with during our supervision and support, and not offloaded on to the client. It is our job to help the client work through his or her feelings about having relapsed, so that he or she feels empowered to try once more.
- Relapse management is exactly like the other parts of counselling: it involves understanding the reasons for a client's behaviour; understanding the central role that a client's expectations and beliefs play in determining his or her behaviour; and enabling a client to learn new, and utilize already learnt, skills.

References and further reading

Laws, D.R. (ed.) (1989) *Relapse Prevention with Sex Offenders*. New York: Guilford.

Marlatt, A. and Gordon, J. (eds) (1985) *Relapse Prevention*. New York: Guilford.

Mason, P. (1989) *Managing Drink*. Birmingham: Aquarius.

Miller, W. (1996) 'What is relapse? Fifty ways to leave the wagon', *Addiction*, 91 (Supplement): S15–S27.

Wanigaratne, S., Wallace, W., Pullin, J., Keaney, F. and Farmer, R. (1990) *Relapse Prevention for Addictive Behaviours: a Manual for Therapists*. Oxford: Blackwell Scientific.

6

Working with Groups

I n many generic agencies there appears to be an implicit rule that 'when in doubt, use a group'. Yet groupwork is highly skilled, different from individual and even couple or family counselling, and comes in many different sorts of package, with different philosophies, aims, and techniques. Even the terms 'group psychotherapy' or 'groupwork' – used to describe services which many agencies say they offer – are misleading, implying a commonality which is not to be found. In fact, these terms are used to encompass almost everything which is not individual, couple, or family work, from a few like-minded colleagues meeting weekly to discuss common concerns, to a large, daily community group meeting in a psychiatric hospital.

Furthermore, all the schools of individual and wider psychotherapy also have adherents who attempt to utilize similar ideas within a group setting. These range from working with individuals within a group setting because it is more economical to see a number of people in the time it takes to see one; to using the group members themselves as the main change agents (believing that a group is greater than the sum of its parts, and that the major sources of change will be the group dynamics and processes within the group); through to using the group as an educational aid to enable the practice of various techniques.

Aims of a group

If one accepts that groups are different, then certain questions must be raised relating to a proposed group.

Who is the group for?

For example, is the group for clients, or for counsellors at the agency, or for supervisors? Or is there a specific group of people within the agency for whom a group is appropriate, such as: women, adolescents, spouses of problem drinkers, family

members, or volunteer counsellors? There will be great differences in style and atmosphere between a group where clients are
referred by the courts in a compulsory and imposed way (a drink-
driving group, say) and a voluntary assertiveness group made up
of clients already in the agency who are keen to attend.

What is the group trying to achieve?

What are the specific goals, aims, and purposes of the group? For
example, is it trying to counsel clients; support previous clients;
deal with specific issues such as relapse management; train clients
to use new skills; educate clients, for example about the effects of
alcohol? Or is it aimed at a different audience altogether, trying to
support counsellors; supervise counsellors' work; train counsellors to use new skills; or supervise and train supervisors?

Working with alcohol-related problems in a group setting

I have said that there is huge variety among the types of group on
offer; Yalom (1986) has suggested that these differences can best
be conceptualized as differences in the surface of the group, in
groups' 'public face'. Beneath their surface differences, however,
groups share the same 'core' features, many of which are among
the advantages of groupwork described below.

The advantages of groups

There are many advantages to seeing clients with alcohol-related
problems in a group. I should add, however, that these advantages are possible, and not certain. As with counselling generally,
how much a client receives will depend fundamentally upon the
skills and commitment of the group leader(s)/facilitator(s). The
advantages marked with an asterisk (*) are those which Yalom
suggested are the components of a core group.

Interpersonal advantages of groupwork

- It can make clients concentrate on others and on what they are
  saying and doing. Clients often appear for help feeling
  worried, uncertain, anxious, angry, defensive, and so on.
  Being counselled in a group setting can push the client out of
  him or herself.
- It can make the client concentrate on his/her own feelings and
  reactions to others.
- It can give the client feedback, if it is an honest group, about
  how he/she comes over to others. (If it is a well-run group,
  this feedback will be non-destructive.)

- It requires clients to give feedback to others about their feelings and reactions, and also about their understanding of the other members' problems and behaviour.
- It requires a willingness not to be the only focus of attention; to share time with others, to let them have a say as well.

Important functions of counselling which can be offered by a group
It can give clients hope and faith in their ability to deal with their problems. This is vital, because high pre-intervention expectations of success are significantly related to positive outcomes. Many people suggest that one of the reasons for the success of AA is that at each meeting at least one person will tell the others that he or she successfully overcame similar problems, showing it is therefore possible (*).

It can impart information about alcohol and alcohol problems to group members, and can provide advice, suggestions, guidance about life problems, and so on (*).

It can provide an environment for learning by imitation. People learn a huge amount via imitation, and a group is an excellent environment for this. Partly this occurs by the counsellor working as the group facilitator: we must model how to act in a positive way within the group (a big responsibility for us as counsellors); and partly via the other group participants (*).

It can help in the development of socializing techniques, due to the modelling and feedback (*).

It can help in the development of insight, which can be of four types:

- How clients are seen initially by others ('You first come across as tense/warm/distant/ etc.').
- What clients are doing to and with others ('Now you have been in the group "x" weeks, your interactions with the other group members seem to be making up some sort of pattern: that is, you often appear rejecting/competitive/etc.').
- Motivational insight into why clients behave as they do ('You come across as so detached – is this because you shy away from intimacy?').
- Developmental insight into how these behaviours might have come about ('Do you think your presentation of yourself as cold and detached could have anything to do with what you have told us about your family as you were growing up, and how you felt continually rejected by them?').

All the above could be done with modifications as well in a non-group setting. There are, however, some functions which can only be done in a group. These include clients learning about the following.

UNIVERSALITY   Clients often feel that the problems which beset them are unique to them, and this is especially the case with clients with alcohol problems. The group can help clients to realize that others have problems which are at least as bad as their own, and may be similar as well. This is especially important as so many individuals with psychological problems generally, and alcohol problems especially, are socially isolated and cannot get this information elsewhere (*).

ALTRUISM   As described above, part of the group ethos is that other members provide feedback and suggestions. Clients therefore have the experience of helping one another by, for example, pointing out each other's strengths and assets. Clients who come into the group feeling demoralized by their failure to deal with their alcohol problems can feel recharged by this – both by being the person who can help others, and by being helped and encouraged by the other group members (*).

FAMILY GROUP   Many clients have had problems in the family (their first group). A good group can show them that groups can be a place for growing and exploring oneself and others, and not just a destructive environment.

The disadvantages of groups

There are six main disadvantages to offering counselling in a group setting.

THERE ARE PEOPLE FOR WHOM A GROUP IS INAPPROPRIATE   To continue the theme introduced earlier in the book of not forcing clients to do things they do not want to, clients who are adamantly against participating in a group should not have to.

Clients will almost always have other problems besides their alcohol problem, and some of these problems will make a group inappropriate – clients who need all the attention; clients who seem cut off from the reality that most of us inhabit; clients who are highly suspicious of other people, are all examples of people about whom I think twice before I include them.

What help is offered must depend on our assessment of the problems which are troubling the client. Groups function best when clients' difficulties are in the interpersonal domain, in that they relate to other people as opposed to attempting to deal with and understand themselves.

We offer help according to our analysis of the nature of the problems, not because our programme dictates that someone with problem 'x' should have a certain type of help or intervention. This view, however, may be at variance with the local court, which might sentence an individual to groupwork, or with your agency who might provide such a groupwork service for the local courts.

WORKING WITH CLIENTS IN A GROUP IS DIFFICULT   Many people do not do this very well. Examining the advantages of groupwork allows the difficulty of our role as facilitators to be highlighted. As counsellors in this context we have to ensure that:

- feedback is given positively and in a non-destructive manner;
- knowledge and information is available and channelled appropriately;
- our behaviour is modelling the correct features for a client to learn; this is difficult for many of us as counsellors, who often, for example, demand self-disclosure from the participants while modelling a tight-lipped impersonal 'professional-helper' façade;
- we provide good modelling of interpersonal socialized behaviour for the participants to copy;
- the group runs smoothly, that participants gain insight, and have a positive experience.

In sum, as facilitators we have to control, encourage, and facilitate the learning and development of about ten somewhat damaged individuals. At the same time, we have to deal with the problem that we, as the facilitators, will be the main focus of the group's feelings, receiving most of the hostility and so on which the members have been storing up. A good idea is to set at the outset the ground rules on how the group will function, and how people will behave and interact with one another, and with us as facilitators.

The range of tasks which need to be undertaken, and the planning necessary to ensure that a group runs well, often means that groups are run badly. Unfortunately, it is very common to find clients who are very fearful of attending a group, due to their negative experiences of previous groups.

ISSUES OF CO-LEADERSHIP/FACILITATION Due to the difficulties in working effectively as a group facilitator, it is advisable for us to work jointly with another counsellor: when one facilitator is interacting with group members, the other can be monitoring and examining the group.

Co-work requires considerable preparation, and often this is not done. This preparation includes such things as deciding when the group should be run, and for how long; and such clearly vital issues as the extent to which the two counsellors' philosophies of change, counselling models, and technique preferences overlap. The two facilitators will also need to agree beforehand who will deal with which sort of problematic situation, so that if one arises, we do not get into the position of talking over one another.

Co-facilitation is very important, so we as counsellors need to ensure that we have met beforehand – probably a number of times – to clarify our areas of agreement and disagreement, and whether or not co-facilitation is a possibility for us. If we do agree that it is possible and advisable, then the issues in the paragraphs above must be sorted out before the group starts.

SOMEONE IN THE AGENCY HAS DECIDED A GROUP SHOULD EXIST Often agencies decide to set up a group and then have to find the clients to fill it. This is a bad system. We need to ask ourselves the question, 'Should this client be offered a group? Is it the best way I can help him or her?' as opposed to asking the question, 'Should this agency be offering groupwork as one of the range of inter-ventions on offer?' The need for a group should be led by the needs of individual clients, not the desire of someone in the agency to do groupwork. As I say above, however, this idea might run counter to the policy of your local court or your local agency, if it has contracted to provide 'groupwork' for court-referred clients.

SUPERVISION Supervision and support are integral parts of counselling; all counsellors should ensure they are well supported and supervised. The problem here is that, although working with clients in groups is different from working individually, many agencies do not offer separate supervision arrangements for groupwork; or cannot locate specifically trained and experienced groupwork supervisors to offer the support. Counsellors starting to work in a group setting need to ensure there are adequate supervision and support arrangements.

OTHER PROBLEMATIC ISSUES Some of the issues outlined in other chapters are particularly important in the group context.

Although we must expect our clients sometimes to drink alcohol before coming for sessions with us (see Chapter 7), this can be especially problematic in a group setting. In an individual setting one can discuss and deal with a client's alcohol consumption, but doing this in a group setting can be very difficult: others who have not drunk can either become very aggressive towards the drinker, or can use this instance as a reason for drinking themselves before future sessions. On the other hand, there are also many occasions when the group can act in very positive and caring ways when someone attends, having drunk. Whatever, as a counsellor or facilitator, we decide to do, however, we must be clear beforehand about our stance, and we must stick to it!

Another potential difficulty exacerbated by the group setting relates to literacy levels. The use of written exercises and written materials is very common within groupwork, and these may reveal undisclosed literacy problems, which can cause immense embarrassment to the individual concerned (as well as to us, as the facilitators). Similar problems can arise in individual work, but then we tend to use written materials less frequently, and also such difficulties are more easily resolved and talked about outside of a group setting.

There are clear advantages and disadvantages to offering help to clients in a group setting. We – or our agency – will have to make a decision as to whether or not one outweighs the other.

Setting up and running a group is a specialist skill. There are a number of excellent training manuals on this topic (for example Saton and Evans, 1982) and potential group facilitators are strongly advised to consult them, and to attend relevant training courses before starting their own groups.

Two examples

I give below two brief examples of how counselling in a group setting is often used with clients with alcohol problems: social skills work, and assertion training.

Social skills

The idea underpinning the teaching of social skills is that everyone has to learn interpersonal skills, which are a necessary precursor to successfully living within society. Some people are lucky enough to have learnt them; others have not been so lucky and have to be taught. Many people with drinking problems have either not learnt social skills, or have learnt a range of inappropriate ones.

Social skills training involves looking closely at the behaviour of individuals who are engaged in social intercourse. These behaviours can be viewed in terms of micro-skills – a series of motor skills which can be taught and learnt, and integrated together; and macro-skills – overall integrated behaviour which can be taught in large bits. The two are often taught together.

The micro-skills often examined include: eye contact (too brief/ too long); use of and invasions of personal space; talking (speed, audibility); listening; posture (legs, fists, openness/closedness).

The macro-skills often examined include:

- greetings – an exercise might involve the group splitting into pairs with each person greeting/being greeted back; and with each giving feedback to the other, for example, commenting on and praising eye contact and voice modulation;
- compliments – an exercise might involve the whole group exchanging compliments;
- small talk – an exercise might involve getting different pairs to, for example, discuss the weather, with the facilitators stressing to the participants that what is said makes no difference; it is the use of the micro-skills which is being practised;
- changing the topic of conversation;
- breaking into other people's conversations;
- improvising in conversations.

Assertion training

Assertion training is concerned with teaching people to express both their positive and negative feelings in an honest, straightforward, and appropriate way. In many ways it is similar to social skills training, and indeed many of the exercises used in social skills training are also used in assertion training. A useful rule of thumb is that if the client does not know what to do, social skills are appropriate; if he or she knows what to do but finds it difficult to do it, assertion training is appropriate. Certainly, in order to be assertive one needs to be socially skilled.

Assertion training is based on a belief that people can alleviate tension by learning to state their desires simply and without apology, and by expressing openly their feelings of resentment, as well as their warmth and cordiality. For that reason, it is as useful for aggressive clients as it is for timid ones.

Besides the social skills exercises, others often used are:

- 'feeling talk' – where group members practise expressing any type of feeling;

- 'facial talk' – where members practise showing expressions which match different emotions;
- disagreeing – with practice gained by expressing contradictory opinions in a non-aggressive way;
- owning – with members practising the use of 'I' as opposed to 'one';
- self-positives – with practice in giving positive self-statements, such as 'I like my sense of humour/taste in clothes';
- accepting compliments – with practise in both exchanging and accepting them: 'Yes, I like this tie/dress too', as opposed to 'Oh, it's years old.'

Key points

- A huge variety of groups exist. If we are thinking of facilitating a group, there are a number of questions which need to be answered in terms of who the group is for, and what the specific objectives are for the group.
- There is a range of reasons both for and against providing help in a group setting, and the particular constellation of factors in any agency must be assessed in order to determine whether or not to offer group-based help.
- Two primary issues that need to be addressed include whether or not the needs of any particular client will be best served by offering and providing help in this form. Groups should not just be offered because someone in the agency likes doing groupwork. The second issue is that groupwork is a difficult and highly skilled activity; counsellors conducting groups should be trained, should always work with a co-facilitator, and should have regular, specific supervision.
- Two examples of skills-based groups are given.

References and further reading

General

Doel, M. and Sawdon, C. (1999) *The Essential Groupworker: Teaching and Learning Creative Groupwork.* London: Kingsley.

Jaques, D. (2000) *Learning in Groups: a Handbook for Improving Group Working* (3rd edn). London: Kogan Page.

Kurtz. L. (1997) *Self-help and Support Groups: a Handbook for Practitioners.* London and Thousand Oaks, CA: Sage.

Levine, J. (2000) *Small Groups.* London: Psychology Press.

Nicols, K. (1976) 'Preparation for membership in a group', *Bulletin of the British Psychological Society,* 29: 353–9.

Nicols, K. and Jenkinson, J. (1991) *Leading a Support Group*. London: Chapman Hall.

Ratigan, B. (1989) 'Counselling in groups', in W. Dryden, D. Charles-Edwards and R. Woolfe (eds), *Handbook of Counselling in Britain*. London: Routledge.

Rose, S. (1986) 'Group methods', in F. Kanfer and A. Goldstein (eds), *Helping People Change* (3rd edn). New York: Pergamon.

Saton, A. and Evans, M. (1982) *Working with Groups*. Salford: Tacade Publications.

Wilson, J. (1995) *How to Work with Self Help Groups: Guidelines for Professionals*. Aldershot: Arena.

Yalom, I. (1986) *The Theory and Practice of Group Psychotherapy* (3rd edn). New York: Basic Books.

PART 3
OTHER IMPORTANT TOPICS

———————— 7 ————————

Dealing with Difficult Situations

So far, this book has implied that counselling problem drinkers is a trouble-free and ordered process, following stages of trust-making, exploration, goal-setting, action, maintenance, and ending; with clients moving through the cycle of change from pre-contemplation to maintenance; with counsellors using a variety of useful assessment and intervention tools; and counsellor and client taking the commonly occurring relapse easily in their stride.

The problem is, of course, that difficulties do sometimes arise. This chapter will examine a number of these problems. First, an examination of a range of difficult situations is offered. Among the situations covered are those dealing with: aggression and violence; clients who have been drinking; clients who are drunk; clients on the telephone; others on the telephone (concerned relative, and so on); invasions of privacy (telephone calls late at night at home); meeting clients in the community or in the pub; requests for money or housing; requests for total confidentiality.

These are followed by a discussion of some common problems concerning clients, ourselves as counsellors, and our agencies. The chapter finishes by examining some particular issues for volunteer counsellors.

Difficult situations

For many of the following situations, the agency within which we work will have policies. The guidelines below are not meant to counter any agency's policy, and when in doubt, we must follow the instructions laid down where we work.

Aggression and violence

In all my years of working with clients with alcohol problems, I have never seen a violent incident in a helping agency – they are actually rather rare. Yet this is the most common issue over which counsellors worry, and over which they need reassurance. Such reassurance is possible: although violence is rare, its frequency can be even further reduced. As with relapse, things can be done to stop a situation becoming violent; and things can be done to defuse it after the situation has reached 'flash-point'.

To stop a situation from becoming violent, always be sure another worker is in the building (or in close proximity if working in a large building). If the agency cannot provide cover – a second person to stay while we are seeing the client – then we should refuse to counsel. Possibly, we might want to break this rule with a well-known client; but it should not be our choice: it should be an agency rule, which we should not be allowed to break.

Ask the agency to install panic buttons in each room, and make sure the room is arranged so we sit near it. Panic buttons are probably not necessary, but they are useful for inspiring confidence in workers. Furthermore, if a situation should ever arise such that the button was necessary, it would be reassuring to know it was there.

We must be very careful if we know that a client has a history of violence.

Understand violence. Violence is similar to drinking, in that it happens for reasons. Usually these are that the client feels frustrated and/or angry. So we must use our counselling skills to join with a client, to make him or her feel understood and valued, and that we are on his or her side. If we do this well, the chances are the client will not feel frustrated or angry with us, and so not be violent with us. We must also pick up on what is happening; on whether the client is starting to appear angry with us; if so, start to take evasive action.

Tell the client what the boundaries of acceptability are. For example, that 'It's OK to shout' (if it is), or 'It's OK to kick a chair over'. This will release the client from worrying about whether or not he or she has exceeded the bounds of acceptability. We must also say what is not acceptable.

To defuse a 'flash-point' situation, comment on the situation rather than ignore it. We should tell the client how we feel: 'I feel you are becoming angry with me. I don't want you to feel annoyed with me.'

Try to deal with the situation, for example ask what we can do to repair the situation: 'What can I do to stop you from feeling annoyed with me?' or what the client wishes from us so that he or she will no longer be angry: 'Is there something you want me to do or say which will stop you feeling annoyed?'

Adopt a one-down position: 'I'm sorry if I've made you angry – what can I do?' is better than, 'Why have you got angry with me? You've misinterpreted what I've said', which might sound as if we are accusing the client of being in the wrong.

Be direct about what we want – if the client has a weapon, ask him or her to put it down; if we want the client to leave now, ask him or her to do so. The best way to do this is to ask nicely, but firmly: 'Please will you put that knife down, or else, I'm sorry, but the session will have to end.'

Do not be too 'counselly'! If the client is shouting, do not be too calm – we need to try to respond to the client in a way which shows we are listening and reacting. This does not mean entering into a shouting match; but a cold, 'clinical' detachment, or an over-soothing vocal style, might inflame the situation. The client needs to know he or she is being listened to and understood and not just being fobbed off as another deranged person.

If the situation deteriorates, we must use our counselling skills, but in a different way. Our task is to contain the situation, which means trying to retain some power and control. We want to stay on the relatively narrow line between being confrontational, which might further inflame the situation, and being too obsequious or scared, which leaves us being powerless. So, we should:

- avoid direct eye contact, which might appear confrontational – it is better to look just below the eyes;
- try not to act scared – sitting rigidly or fidgeting. If we are scared, we should try to control our breathing, and try to sit relatively still – although not motionless, which might signify aggression to some people;
- try to divert the client's attention in a subtle way – 'I really feel like a cup of coffee now; do you want one?' or 'I just need to go to the toilet';
- not touch the client – physical contact when adrenalin is high is a mistake.

Davies (1989) examines in detail how to prevent assault on professional helpers.

The client who has been drinking

The alcohol field is in some ways a very odd one. Although agencies which deal with depression or bereavement do not require clients to be un-depressed or non-grieving before offering help, many agencies dealing with drinking problems do require clients to be abstinent before they are prepared to help them. Some agencies require abstinence for some time (two weeks in some cases), and most demand abstinence at least on the day that the client attends for counselling. My view is rather different.

Many clients find coming for help an anxiety-raising experience; many others are highly ambivalent about coming in the first place; it is not surprising that many of them find a drink helps them to get the courage or commitment to attend. Furthermore, some clients who are very dependent on alcohol need to have some alcohol in their system to stop them experiencing fits or other serious withdrawal effects. Certainly, one of the tasks of counselling these clients will be to help them to reach the stage where they can come without the help of alcohol; but to insist on this as a first step seems to me rather rigid.

When a client does come, having drunk, I will usually comment on it, and use it within the session: 'Why did you feel the need?', and so on. Often clients will try to deny they have had a drink, because they are scared that if they admit it, they will have to leave. Once we have reassured them, they will usually open up.

I also discuss with clients generally at some stage the fact that they are attempting to change their behaviour for themselves, not for me. I tell them, therefore, that I will always accept what they say to me as the truth – if they tell me less than the truth, or are 'economical with the truth', that is fine. There are always reasons for people to behave in the ways they do, and if they do not want to tell me something, that is their prerogative. If any harm comes as a result of it, it is not going to harm me, only them. The issue of a client having drunk will almost always arise anyway, in that it is good practice to ask the client to produce a drinking diary at every session.

The client who is drunk

This relates to the previous issue, although it is rather different. Much depends on what we mean by 'drunk'. I try to assess how useful it might be to have a session with a client in the state they are currently in. If the client has had a bit of 'Dutch courage' to help him or her come, but is not the worse for wear, then I will see him or her for a session; but if he or she is intoxicated, I will not.

Now, this does not mean I ask the client to leave immediately, which might be very damaging to the counselling relationship. Instead, I might sit the client down, offer a cup of coffee, have a bit of a chat, and then move him or her on, perhaps having made an appointment for the next day, written it down, and put it in the client's pocket. It is surprising how many clients do return for appointments made while they are intoxicated.

Clients on the telephone

Telephone counselling is a subject in its own right. What we do depends on the client and their particular difficulties. We have to use slightly more of our verbal than our non-verbal counselling skills, as there is not much point nodding and smiling on the phone! That being said, our facial expressions do alter the tone of our voice, and even the way we say things. Other than using more vocal skills, however, the messages concerning telephone coun-selling are the same as for face-to-face work: there is no point in trying to counsel someone who is very drunk, very angry, or aggressive, so try to talk them down. Davies and Raistrick (1981) have a useful section in their book on how to deal with many different sorts of telephone call.

Other people on the telephone

Chapter 10 deals with the issue of relatives in detail. Two points need to be made here, however. The first is the important issue of confidentiality: we must not be seduced into discussing a current client with a relative, or with anyone else (see p. 128ff.). The second is that it is totally appropriate to deal with and counsel a relative: they are, or should be, legitimate clients in any agency within which we work.

Invasions of privacy

Many agencies and counsellors have strict rules about not giving their home telephone numbers to clients. I do the opposite: it is rare that I do not give my home number to clients, and this is for clear philosophical reasons. If we are trying to help clients we must be available to help them when they need us, and not just whenever we happen to be in our offices; and we must treat clients in the way we would want to be treated ourselves – as people who can be trusted, not as children who cannot be trusted with our home phone numbers in case they misuse them.

Of course, having asked clients to phone us in an emergency, we cannot define such calls as an invasion of privacy. But some-times clients do misuse this trust, and then we get the invasions of privacy we are concerned with. Sometimes clients just telephone us for a chat, thoughtlessly: recently, I was telephoned at mid-night by a new client who wanted to arrange a further appoint-ment. We quickly agreed that he would telephone again the

following day at a somewhat less nocturnal time. Also, clients'
views of what is an emergency sometimes differ from our view or
from the views of our families!

As with other phone calls, the job is to help in whatever way we
can to enable the client to cope and get through the situation until
the next day. It is, however, legitimate to say it is not a convenient
time to call, and to explain that we would rather be telephoned at
night only in an emergency. Much, of course, depends on our
assessment of the degree of urgency the call warrants.

Meeting problem-drinking clients outside

Act naturally. We do not want the client to feel we are ignoring
him or her; but on the other hand, we do not want to embarrass
the client by showing we know him or her in a context where the
client would have to explain how he or she knew us.

If meeting is a possibility, a good plan is to discuss this with the
client in a session. I work out with the client what he or she would
like me to do. I also make certain the client realizes that if I am out
for a drink or a social evening with friends or with my partner, I
will not have the time, nor would it be appropriate, for us to have
a long chat.

There are times when this does not work. We may meet a client
with whom we have been working who is relapsing. He or she
may become abusive or nasty in one way or another. If it is
possible, a sensible policy is to leave and go to another pub.
Whatever happens, we should not get involved in an argument
with the client.

Requests for money or housing

It is important to be very clear with clients over what we can and
cannot do, which depends to a large extent on the agency within
which we are counselling. For example, many social services
agencies see it as their job to intercede with other welfare organizations on the client's behalf (with housing departments or with
the Department of Social Security in the UK), whereas other
agencies do not. As with so many other issues, we must be guided
by our agency's policies. But in general, we must be clear that we
are working with a client as a counsellor, not as someone who will
be able to provide material help. Enabling the client to develop his
or her skills so that an approach to a social welfare agency such as
a housing department will be more effective, is more of a counselling task than doing it ourselves.

Requests for total confidentiality

Most agencies have similar rules concerning confidentiality. One important element is that information which a client gives us is 'confidential to the agency', as opposed to being totally confidential between us and the client. This is a sensible rule: without it, supervision would be impossible, as would writing up notes, which remain the property of the agency, not of the individual counsellor.

Clients will sometimes ask us to breach this rule, and to keep things totally confidential. This pressure should be resisted. Saying we will do it, and then telling other people, is unacceptable – we cannot expect clients to be honest if we are not. And accepting information which cannot be discussed in supervision stores up considerable problems for us as counsellors. After all, what information is it that cannot be shared? Presumably material that is potentially damaging or embarrassing, such as child abuse, which is precisely the sort of information that may need to be discussed in supervision.

Other issues of confidentiality

Confidentiality issues require particular care. Clients may tell us things that could be damaging for other people to know. They entrust this information to us, and expect us to respect it. The usual confidentiality rule is that material is confidential within an agency – it can be discussed within the agency, with others who are part of the agency, but not with outsiders. But there are often areas which are less well worked out. For example, issues arise concerning the exchange of information with other professionals:

- if the client is on a probation order, and the probation officer wishes to know how the client is doing;
- if the client has been referred by his or her employer, who now wants to know whether or not to proceed with disciplinary action;
- if the doctor telephones, wanting to discuss the best way of integrating his or her home detoxification plans with our counselling.

A good policy is to not discuss any information relating to any particular client with any outsider, without first having received the client's permission. We could discuss the general issue of detoxification, for example, but not the specific one unless the client has agreed that we can pass on the information.

But this raises further problems. If when the doctor or the employer telephones we respond by saying, 'I am sorry but we cannot discuss our clients with anyone unless we have permission from the client to do so', we are implicitly agreeing that the client is attending the agency. So even in refusing to pass across information, we may be breaching confidentiality. A truly confidential agency will keep secret even the fact that a person is a client of the agency.

On the other hand, the idea of any of our agencies being 'a truly confidential' one is becoming less likely, and indeed less of an issue. In the ten years between the first and second editions of this book, thinking about confidentiality has moved on. Increasingly, agencies are working together to a greater extent to plan both the care and the pathways of care for people with alcohol problems. 'Sharing of information' protocols are now much more common, where what information is to be shared, and the circumstances of that sharing, are clearly laid out. Increasingly, both shop-front/ walk-in agencies and agencies which cater primarily for self-referred clients are accepting referrals from others (such as GPs). By doing this they are also moving into a scenario where the normal rules of medical information-sharing hold. By this, I mean that

- a GP will normally expect a written response after referring someone;
- they will expect this response to contain the results of our assessment, and our suggestions for what should happen next;
- they will expect that these suggestions will be either that we will go on to offer help or counselling to this person (in which case the GP will want to know our intervention plan and our estimate of how long the intervention will take); or, if we are not proposing to take on the client, the GP will want our suggestions for how they should plan the further management of the client.

So the older ideas of complete client confidentiality are starting to break down, and information is being shared more freely. My view on this is that this greater sharing is potentially a good thing, as long as the guiding principle is that the sharing is done, and decisions about what information is shared are taken, clearly and explicitly in the client's best interests, and on a 'need to know' basis.

The issues over confidentiality are even further exacerbated when family members become involved. Sometimes a spouse may suspect that his or her partner is attending the agency, and may telephone to find out; yet often a client may not want his or her spouse to know that counselling is going on. On the other hand, family members can often be key allies in helping people move and change, and excluding them from knowing that counselling is going on, and what has been agreed in counselling, may mean that the plans made within the counselling sessions are less likely to succeed.

The telephone rings at the agency where we work. Mr Smith wants to leave a message for his wife, who he thinks is coming in for an appointment later. What should we answer? On the one hand, if Mrs Smith has been open with her husband about coming, then it might seem churlish to refuse to take a message. And what exactly would we say to refuse? On the other hand, accepting the message means the agency is revealing that Mrs Smith is a client; and she may have come to the agency exactly because it said it offered a confidential service.

The situation becomes even more complex if two members of the same family are seen at the same agency, either by the same counsellor, or by two different ones who share the same supervision group. In these situations, or when another professional helper gives us information about a client in a referral letter, but does not wish the client to know that this information has been passed on, we are party to information about a client, some of which we might not have acquired directly from that client:

One agency uses group supervision. Counsellor A, seeing male client B, discovered that someone else in the supervision group was concurrently seeing B's wife. B did not know his wife was also a client in the agency, and the wife feared he would be violent with her if her visits were discovered. Both counsellors discussed their respective clients in the group. In a subsequent session, counsellor A said something which client B claimed had not come from him.

Such situations mean it is imperative we have a system whereby we can separate out information gained directly from the client from knowledge gained from other sources. The most useful system is for us not to see two clients from the same family, and to change supervision groups if someone else in the group needs to discuss material which might affect our relationship with our client. I say more about how to work with family members in Chapter 10.

Common problems and difficulties

The time taken to move through the six stages of counselling – developing trust, exploration, goal-setting, action, maintenance, and ending – varies with different people. We always need to use the first skills; though apparently the most simple, they have been shown to be the most effective. Nevertheless, even though our skills develop and our experience grows, some clients never seem able to move at all. No matter how skilled we become at, for example, confronting, some people do not change.

Working with clients with alcohol problems is often a cyclical process where people may make one move forward and then seem to go back again. As counsellors, we may have to stick it out, if the clients will, until they are ready to shift on a more permanent basis.

Three sorts of problems may occur: those concerning clients; ourselves as counsellors; and the administration or management of the agency in which we work.

Problems concerning clients

CLIENTS ARE OFTEN AMBIVALENT ABOUT WANTING HELP   Even those who are not ambivalent will sometimes want something that will work quickly, some magic cure, rather than slow-moving intervention. Even those who are not ambivalent and who recognize the need for change in lifestyle and in thinking will sometimes shy away from looking at themselves, because it can be painful.

All these things lead people to be defensive, which can manifest itself in a variety of ways: silences, denial of the problem, aggression, worries about confidentiality, getting depressed and stuck and seeming to prefer that to failure, drinking before the session, and so on. It is important to realize that the reason these things appear is often a fear of changing – fear of the unknown.

CLIENTS OFTEN TRY TO GO TOO FAST OR EXPECT TOO MUCH   Even if they realize that change is up to them rather than it being up to us to produce a magic cure, the client may feel disappointed at the slow pace of change, or at how family or employers are not taking their changes seriously.

CLIENTS PROJECT OR TRANSFER THEIR FEELINGS ONTO US *Projection* is when clients project their own current feelings or fears on to us. Sometimes this leads to clients claiming they are picking these feelings up from us – for example, they may tell us that they feel we are angry with them when in fact they are angry with us. Sometimes we may be left at the end of a session with feelings which are 'left over' from the session – for example, feeling very anxious, having seen a very anxious client, or feeling low after seeing a depressed client. *Transference* occurs when clients transfer their feelings about important people in their current or past lives on to us. A client might start loving us or hating us, not for what we have said or done, but because of who we represent to him or her. A related issue is *counter-transference*, which occurs when we as counsellors transfer our feelings about important people in our lives on to our clients, and relate to them because in some unconscious way they remind us of a parent, say, or some other key figure.

Projection, transference, and counter-transference can be difficult to handle – or even to perceive – but we must be aware of them as possibilities, and feed back to clients (or to our supervisors in relation to counter-transference) when we feel they are happening. Clients generally are unaware they are doing these things – they are unconscious rather than deliberate – and as with everything else, one should feed these things back as a hypothesis to be tested, rather than as a definitive statement or interpretation. Hence it is always better to say, 'I'm feeling a bit uncomfortable at the moment, and I'm wondering whether you are angry with me?', as opposed to making a categorical statement such as, 'You are angry with me.' It is my experience that the latter tends to make clients defensive rather than willing to explore whether or not they are actually angry.

CLIENTS MAY GET TOO INVOLVED WITH US AS COUNSELLORS They may become overdependent, for example, or sexually interested. Generally, the client needs to be reminded, caringly but firmly, that the relationship we have is a professional one and that it will end within the foreseeable future. If my practice (outlined in Chapter 3) is followed, of offering five-session renewable contracts, the client will already be well aware of the time-limited nature of our sessions.

CLIENTS MAY ARRIVE HAVING BEEN DRINKING Or clients may arrive intoxicated. These situations have been examined above.

'NON-DRINKING DRINKERS'   The ethos of this book is that people do things for reasons. The corollary of this is that if people simply deal with the overt problem – the drinking – without dealing with the underlying issues – the reasons why the person has allowed his or her drinking to become problematic – then that person's problems are unlikely to disappear.

We as counsellors may be confronted with a client who is no longer drinking but who fears their underlying problems have not been satisfactorily dealt with. A person may present him or herself to an agency having already taken action – in this case, having stopped drinking – but fearing that the maintenance phase will be problematic because the reasons for the drinking have not yet been tackled.

As counsellors, we have to use a mixture of techniques. We need specifically to help the client withstand at-risk situations, and generally to explore further the functions of drinking, clarifying what has been lost as a result of ceasing to drink. An effective way of doing this is to pose the questions, 'What would you be seeking to get by returning to drinking; and in what ways could these advantages be gained from means other than drinking?'

DEALING WITH THE DISCLOSURE OF TRAUMATIC EVENTS   As we know, people develop problems with drinking for many reasons. One common reason relates to traumatic past experiences. Counselling may impact on this in two ways. First, as the client starts to trust you, he or she may feel enabled and empowered to start to reveal to you the extent of these traumatic events. Second, the client may in fact not consciously recall at the start of counselling that traumatic event(s) had been experienced, but as the client starts to both relax and reflect within the counselling sessions, he or she may begin to recall such events. Such disclosures will often be very painful and traumatic for our clients, and they may well be very traumatic for us as well.

We are there to help and empower our clients, and hence to support them through these traumatic memories. I recommend that a particularly useful piece of further training that agencies should put on would relate to techniques for dealing with PTSD – post-traumatic stress disorder. On the other hand, however, we need to help our clients live in the present and the future, and not in the past. We need to help them realize that the past has fashioned them into the people they are at the moment, but that they can take control of their lives and create the future for themselves. They need to know that none of us need to be controlled and restricted by the past – the past is not a strait-jacket from which we cannot escape.

DEALING WITH THE FEELINGS BROUGHT UP BY COUNSELLING   One of the effects of drinking is that it helps block out one's awareness of all sorts of things. One of the effects of counselling is that, when we help people start to better understand their behaviour, they start to become more aware of past and current behaviour (as in the example above, of traumatic past events). Counselling allows people to take the time to start to reflect, and when they do that, it is often the case that uncomfortable and sometimes painful feelings emerge. Clients commonly become upset, for example, or they often become very ashamed of their past behaviour when they think about what they did when they were drinking to excess.

One major difficulty is that very often clients have few ways of coping with these and other uncomfortable feelings other than drinking. This may mean that, as a result of counselling, our clients tend to drink more heavily after our counselling sessions; or the very fact of undertaking the counselling increases the chances of someone relapsing – a bit of a double-bind both for us as counsellors and for our clients!

My approach is to be very open about these issues with clients. One of the tasks of counselling is certainly to help people get in touch with and vent their feelings. But it is equally true that another key task of counselling is to explore with clients what they do when they are upset. A key role here for us as counsellors is to help and enable the client to develop new skills (other than drinking) for dealing with these painful, uncomfortable, and difficult feelings. And we as counsellors need to be very alert to how our clients are feeling (before, during, and after) as we explore with them potentially painful past events.

Finally, we also need to be aware that the issue of double-bind mentioned above may have even worse consequences. There is a strong association between drinking and both deliberate self-harm and suicide – people with alcohol problems are far more likely than the general population both to attempt suicide and to succeed in these suicide attempts. The double-bind may be that the memories or feelings emerging are extremely painful, and yet the client is committed to not continuing to cope in the ways that he or she did – i.e. drinking. But with no alternatives available, for some people suicide seems to be the only viable route. Other clients do relapse into drinking, and it is then that the juxtaposition between having committed themselves to not drinking, and then having actually drunk to excess again, means that they feel so guilty and such failures that they decide to harm themselves.

Again, my approach is to talk about these risks with my clients, and work with them to develop a sufficiently strong relationship for them to feel that they can come back to tell me how they are feeling, or that they have relapsed, as opposed to feeling that they have to cope (or not) on their own.

If we need to see our client's spouse in order to help effectively, we may find it difficult to get him/her along. This might be a defensive reaction on the part of the client, or it might be indicative of a problem in the relationship (Chapter 10).

How we react to all of the problems outlined above is important. Whatever we do gives our client some message about our feelings for him/her and our attitudes to his or her behaviour, so the message we want to give needs to be carefully thought out.

Problems concerning ourselves as counsellors

There are a number of skills issues that arise in counselling which can cause us difficulty. The list that follows is not exhaustive, but they are all problems which have recently occurred with counsellors whom I know, and they underline the importance of counsellors continually updating their training. The topics of this updating should include:

- structuring sessions, planning, goal-setting. Many people find the degree of clarification of purposes and goals, and working towards achieving them, difficult. This is especially so for new counsellors, and getting counsellors to practise timing sessions, and setting timings for how long they think they wish to take to cover certain topics, might be useful. In general, however, we must take our timings from the client rather than following a pre-set plan;
- when to work with spouse or parents; joint sessions or individual ones; when and if to use information gleaned in sessions with parents or spouse in sessions with clients;
- time-keeping problems. As counsellors sometimes find it difficult to structure the session, it can be difficult to know when the end of the session has arrived;
- how and when to terminate counselling;
- family counselling: is it necessary, and, if so, what skills are needed?
- how directive we should be as counsellors. For example, if someone is in a high-risk job, should we advise them to change?

- deciding when a counsellor should refer. How do we know if this is a case which we cannot handle?
- how and when to use controlled drinking.

The above are all legitimate issues to ask for training on. It is the responsibility of the agency to organize training; but it is partially our responsibility to delineate what that training should cover.

There also exist a number of issues which are best dealt with during supervision. These relate to our feelings about counselling, and often to our defensiveness. Some of these issues include:

- trying to go too fast or expecting too much;
- feeling unskilled and inexperienced;
- feeling useless and impotent: confusing our own effectiveness with the enormity of the problem;
- feeling that we keep coming up against a brick wall; that we cannot get to the deep feelings;
- feeling angry and rejected when a client does not return;
- feeling depressed and stuck, and afraid of trying something new;
- feeling worried about client dependency;
- becoming too involved with the client: only we know the client and only we can put it right;
- feeling worried about the destructive effects of counselling. Sometimes change is not in the direction expected either by the client or by us. We sometimes feel responsible if marriages break up, and so on;
- what to do about feelings of attraction (or repulsion) for clients. How separate can we keep our own feelings from the counselling relationship?

There are two stages through which we as counsellors need to work. First, we have to *be aware of our own feelings*, in order to distinguish between what the client is putting into the session and what we are putting in. Our job is to help the client to deal with his or her feelings, not with ours – except if the client needs to understand that the way that he or she says or does something causes others to react in a certain way. Here it may be appropriate to discuss our own feelings.

Having become aware of our feelings, and having placed them to one side within the counselling session, the second stage, of *understanding and dealing with them*, must be addressed. As counsellors, we need support. We need encouragement, challenge, warmth, empathy, genuineness, and an opportunity to talk about counselling generally, and our cases specifically. Supervision is vital, and it must be of a sufficient quality to enable these and other issues to be safely and effectively addressed.

Problems concerning agencies

All sorts of difficulties can arise between ourselves as counsellors and the agencies within which we work. Three types of problem frequently occur: those connected with a mismatch of values or philosophies; those concerned with a lack of clarity as to what to do in certain situations; and those concerned with inadequacies which we perceive in what is actually offered.

Mismatch of values arises when agencies have clear policies with which we disagree. These include agencies which forbid, or disapprove of, offering controlled drinking; or accord relatives of problem drinkers a low priority as clients, or even refuse to deal with them; or refuse to see clients if they have been drinking at all; or disallow home visits; and so on.

Other issues might arise over how the agency deals with us as counsellors. For example, the agency might have a clear policy on the provision of supervision, but we might feel that, to take a common instance, half an hour of once-weekly supervision with a caseload of 40 clients is inappropriate.

Where there is a disparity between our philosophy and that of the agency within which we work, we have two choices: either leave the agency, or attempt to change the corporate view. The latter method is often not as difficult as it sounds: many agencies are open to suggestions from those who work for them. One voluntary agency with which I am familiar has two large meetings a year for everyone who works in the agency. The first consists of agenda-setting: policy and practice issues are discussed which determine the way the agency works, and its priorities for the future year; and the second, six months later, evaluates progress made towards these goals.

Lack of clarity concerns topics over which we cannot disagree because the agency position is unclear. Common examples include issues around note-taking and record-keeping, such as: exactly how does the agency wish us to keep notes – what format should we adopt, what style, how long should they be, why has the agency provided no training on this issue? When should these notes be written – during the session, immediately after, at the end of the day? Where should these records be kept – at the agency, at home? Should we keep different notes for the super-visor and for the agency?

Furthermore, sometimes the preliminary answers to these questions are contradictory. I can recall one agency that had a rule stating that records could not be taken out of the building, and had to be written up immediately after the session. The agency also offered counselling sessions in a variety of outposts and doctors' surgeries, which placed counsellors in a double-bind situation: the clients' records were stored in the agency building, yet the clients were seen elsewhere, and the records could not be transported.

Such anomalies should be raised with the agency and clear policies need to be written. When in doubt, we should put forward a sensible policy ourselves.

Inadequacies in what is provided occur when the agency is clear, and we do not disagree with the policies, but we find they are not carried through in practice. One common example relates to low levels of communication. For most agencies, we, the counsellors, are their life-blood. Frequently these agencies talk about the importance of open communication within the organization. Yet all too often decisions are made by people who have long since ceased to counsel clients. And often we do not get to hear about the decisions until after they have been taken, and then only on some internal grapevine.

Another common example relates to supervision being inadequate. This occurs in two ways. First, if the supervisor simply offers a quick chat as opposed to a planned and structured supervision session. 'Is everything going all right with your cases?' is not a substitute for proper supervision. The second failure arises if the supervisor becomes more interested in us retelling the case history than in enabling us to clarify what we are doing with the client, what our direction should be, what issues are emerging for us which might interfere with our counselling, or which need dealing with, and so on.

With both examples, and other situations where what is provided is inadequate, we need to take strong action to redress these problems. We should not be expected to work in agencies where our work or we ourselves are not respected.

Particular problems for the volunteer counsellor

There is a variety of particular issues which arise when the counselling which we offer is voluntary, as opposed to being paid for by the agency. Some of these concern people's perceptions of what being a volunteer means; others relate to the part-time nature of most volunteer counselling.

Volunteers

RELATIONSHIPS WITH OTHER PROFESSIONAL STAFF   Many other workers
are rather negative about those of us who work as volunteer
counsellors. These views result from a confusion over the two
meanings of 'volunteer' – unpaid on the one hand, and unprofessional on the other. Many paid workers, originally trained in
one of the professions, see volunteers as being 'unprofessional'.
This partly stems from the Victorian view of volunteers as middle-
class, middle-aged, female, do-gooders. But a counsellor who has
been trained via the Volunteer Alcohol Counsellor Training
Scheme (VACTS) programme should be able to easily dispel these
views.

Any course associated with the VACTS scheme has met the
minimum standards set by the scheme (Alcohol Concern, 1991,
1992a, 1992b), which cover:

- counsellor selection and assessment throughout training;
- qualifications and experience of trainers and supervisors;
- content of the instructional part of the course;
- practical counselling experience which the counsellors need to
  undergo;
- quantity and quality of counselling experience, supervision,
  and continued training of counsellors;
- how counsellors are managed by the agency.

Volunteer counsellors trained under the VACTS scheme are
probably at least as well trained and supervised as any 'professional' worker. Further information about the current VACTS
scheme is given in Appendix 1, on facilities in the UK providing
help for people with alcohol problems.

Furthermore, because volunteer counsellors in the VACTS
scheme have to be re-accredited at regular intervals, which can
only happen if they have received the required quality and
quantity of further training and supervision, there is a continual
need for the agency to provide a minimum standard of these
elements. Most other professionals do not have similar require-
ments (although the notion of mandatory 'continual professional
development' is growing in many professions), and hence are
often the first to suffer at times of pressure.

The key issue, therefore, is to show that we are as 'professional'
as any of the other workers. One easy way of dealing with this is
simply not informing workers we are volunteers, by, for example,

signing letters as 'Counsellor' as opposed to 'Volunteer Coun-sellor'. After all, do other workers discuss their pay with us when they write letters? The issue of remuneration for our work is of no concern to anyone other than the agency who pays us (or not!) and ourselves.

This is a slightly more complex issue when dealing with paid staff who work within the same agency, in that they will probably know we work voluntarily. But we must again ensure that these workers realize the standards to which we are trained.

We might also wish them to realize that the evidence from many evaluations of the outcome of counselling is quite clear: there is little difference between the success rates obtained by professional workers such as psychologists, doctors, and social workers, and the results obtained by para-professionals and volunteers. Where differences do exist, though, the better results are obtained by the volunteers, not the professionals (this work is summarized in Derek Milne's recent book *Social Therapy*, and see also the work by Faust and Zlotnick (1995) and Christensen and Jacobson (1994) listed at the end of this chapter).

ATTITUDES OF CLIENTS   Again, many clients might have negative views about being seen by a volunteer, feeling this is an inferior alternative to being seen by a professional. The same answer applies – why should the client need to know the arrangements between us and the agency within which we are working? There are, of course, times when it might be helpful for a client to know that we are helping them not simply because it is a job which pays the mortgage, but because we actually want to do it. It is not that we should never tell others that we are volunteers, it is just not necessary to do so in all cases.

PROFESSIONAL JEALOUSY AND DEFENSIVENESS   The points above relating to how well volunteers are trained, and the evidence that volunteers seem to be more effective than professionals, sometimes serve to alienate paid 'professional' workers, who feel threatened by how skilled volunteers are in relation to themselves. This is not surprising: many professional workers have remark-ably little practical training in the skills of counselling, and even less in the specifics of counselling problem drinkers.

The solution is for us to use our counselling skills by informing other workers about our training in a way that stops them from seeing us as inferior, yet without making them feel threatened because of their own lack of training.

Part-time work

A number of difficulties arise if we work with an agency on a part-time basis, and these are exacerbated if we are also working as volunteers.

LIAISON WITH OTHER PROFESSIONALS   As counsellors, we will often need to contact other workers, such as a doctor or probation officer, and they will often need to contact us. Problems can arise when we are contacted and we are not there. It can lead to these other workers becoming exasperated, or denigrating the agency as 'unprofessional'. It can also lead to the agency trying to restrict whom we see to certain categories of client, or to appointing a keyworker who is not a part-time volunteer.

There are two easy solutions to this. As noted above, we should simply sign our letters 'Counsellor' and not inform people of the fact that we work voluntarily. And, if we can regularize our hours with the agency, and inform other professionals who might need to contact us of what these hours are, then there should be no problem. Increasingly, due to job-sharing, people are having to learn how to deal with part-time staff.

ACCESS TO SECRETARIAL SERVICES   Often part-timers seem to have the lowest priority when it comes to secretarial services. The solution to this is to clearly make our case that we need these resources in the same way as do other workers, and to get agreement that we can use them.

RECORD-KEEPING AND WHERE RECORDS SHOULD BE KEPT AND WRITTEN UP   Being part-time should not pose any more problems than being full-time. If the agency requires notes to be written before leaving the premises, this can be carried out as well by a part-timer.

Key points

- Some difficulties arising in counselling concern situations which are difficult to deal with; others concern common problems which counsellors report with clients, with ourselves as counsellors, and with our agencies. Volunteers sometimes have special difficulties.
- The most common issue over which counsellors worry is dealing with aggression and violence. When counselling clients with alcohol difficulties, violence is rare, but the

incidence can be even further reduced. There are things that can be done to stop a situation ever becoming violent; and things that can be done to defuse it after the situation has reached 'flash-point'.

- Many clients find it difficult to come for help, and find that having a drink helps. There is no harm in this, although an aim in the long term would be to help the client to do difficult things without needing alcohol. Whether or not we should see a client who is drunk depends on the extent to which it might be useful to have a session with him or her at that time.

- When dealing with others, especially relatives, on the telephone, we must not be seduced into discussing a client. But the relative is, or should be, a legitimate client of any agency within which we work.

- Most agencies have similar rules concerning confidentiality. One important element is that information which a client gives us is 'confidential to the agency', as opposed to being totally confidential between the counsellor and the client. Clients will sometimes pressure us to breach this rule, and to keep things totally confidential, which should be resisted. Confidentiality issues also arise concerning the exchange of information with other professionals. This problem is exacerbated when family members become involved. We need to be very clear about what can be said if a relative contacts the agency.

- Many counsellors report common problems and difficulties concerning clients. How we react to all of these is important. Whatever we do gives our client some message, and so the message we want to give must be carefully thought out.

- As counsellors we also have difficulties which relate to ourselves rather than our clients. Some of these relate to skills we might not possess; and others relate to dealing with the feelings that counselling engenders. These should be dealt with via continued training and supervision.

- There are all sorts of difficulties which can arise between ourselves as counsellors and the agencies within which we work. Three types of problem frequently occur: those connected with a mismatch of values or philosophies; those concerned with a lack of clarity as to what to do in certain situations; and those concerned with inadequacies which we perceive in what is actually offered.

- A variety of particular issues arise when the counselling we offer is voluntary as opposed to being paid for by the agency. Some of these problems concern people's perception of what being a volunteer means; others relate to the part-time nature of most voluntary counselling. Both of these types of difficulty can be dealt with.

References and further reading

Alcohol Concern VACTS: Doherty, C., Hoare, I. and Velleman, R. (1991) *Training Volunteer Alcohol Counsellors: Training Guidelines*. London: Alcohol Concern VACTS.

Alcohol Concern VACTS: Doherty, C., Jones, K. and Owen, H. (1992a) *Training Volunteer Alcohol Counsellors: Involving Volunteer Counsellors*. London: Alcohol Concern VACTS.

Alcohol Concern VACTS: Wood-Bevan, M., Doherty, C. and Sainsbury, E. (1992b) *Training Volunteer Alcohol Counsellors: Supervising Volunteer Counsellors*. London: Alcohol Concern VACTS.

Christensen, A. and Jacobson, N. (1994) 'Who (or what) can do psychotherapy: status and challenge of non-professional therapies', *Psychological Science*, 5: 8–14.

Davies, I. and Raistrick, D. (1981) *Dealing with Drink*. London: BBC.

Davies, W. (1989) 'The prevention of assault on professional helpers', in K. Howells and C. Hollin (eds), *Clinical Approaches to Violence*. Chichester: Wiley.

Faust, D. and Zlotnick, C. (1995) 'Another Dodo bird verdict? Revisiting the comparative effectiveness of professional and paraprofessional therapists', *Clinical Psychology and Psychotherapy*, 2: 157–67.

Milne, D. (1999) *Social Therapy: A Guide to Social Support Interventions for Mental Health Practitioners*. Chichester: Wiley.

'Dual Diagnosis' or 'Co-morbidity': Working with People with More Than One Problem

I have placed these two terms – 'dual diagnosis' and 'co-morbidity' – in quotes, because I dislike both of them. They are highly medicalized, and refer to medical processes and medical concepts which are very out of step with the counselling ideas expressed throughout this book. On the other hand, unfortunately, both terms are regularly used, and there is no readily understandable alternative to them as yet – certainly, terms such as 'people with more than one problem' or 'people with both alcohol problems and mental health difficulties' are both far more long-winded, and are not useful shorthand in the ways that these other two terms are. So, under protest, I have used them!

In many ways working with people with more than one problem is something that we always do as alcohol counsellors. Remarkably few people attend for help with a pure alcohol problem, with no other concomitant problems. As I outlined in Chapter 2, dealing with individuals with alcohol problems involves addressing two distinct but related areas, and counsellors will need to deal with both. One concerns the individual's use of drink *per se*; the second concerns other difficulties which connect in some way with the alcohol use. So it is common for people to have other difficulties – relationship problems, health problems, legal problems, work problems. Some of these are caused by the drinking, some may pre-date the drinking (and indeed may be a partial cause of it), some may be exacerbated by the drinking, and some may be unrelated to the drinking.

In these situations we need to help clients work out the relative importance of these different problems, clarify which are the most pressing or the ones that they wish to deal with first, and then decide if we are the best people to help them to deal with these problems. Hence if someone decides that dealing with their bereavement is the most pressing problem, we need to be clear if we are the best person to help this client at this time, or whether he or she needs to seek specialized bereavement counselling first, and only deal with the alcohol issues later.

Of course it is very rarely as simple as this, and usually a number of problems need to be dealt with at the same time (or in parallel at any rate); and we as counsellors will have views as to which problem may need to be dealt with first. It is completely appropriate for us as counsellors to put our own viewpoints forward, explaining why we think the way we do, but then to empower the client to make the best decision that he or she can at that time.

There are three particular instances relating to these 'more than one' problems that I want to briefly cover in this chapter. These are when someone has problems with both alcohol and other drugs; with both alcohol and serious mental health difficulties; and with both alcohol and more common mental health problems such as anxiety and depression.

Alcohol and other drugs

There are increasing numbers of people presenting for help with problems with both alcohol and other drugs, both within the UK and elsewhere. This is not surprising. The overall consumption of illicit drugs in the UK (and elsewhere in the Western world) has been rising sharply over the past three decades. As we saw in Chapter 1, the amount of alcohol-related problems in a country are closely linked with the overall amount of alcohol consumed in that country, and the same is the case with illicit drugs – the higher the consumption of drugs in a country, the more people will start to develop problems with them.

As far as counselling people with both alcohol and other drug problems is concerned, three points need to be made.

First, the issues around counselling people with drug problems are very similar to those with alcohol problems, and the techniques we use to help people are also very similar. Clearly there may be extra difficulties over the illicit nature, and the costs, of the drugs, and both of these issues may mean that problems with the criminal justice system are more common in cases where drugs (as opposed to only alcohol) are involved. But the essential similarity remains. As I said in Chapter 2, counselling clients with alcohol problems requires good general counselling skills, plus specific knowledge about alcohol so that we as counsellors understand some of the issues, and also so that we feel confident in dealing

with people with these problems. The same is true with counselling people with drug problems. Anyone who reads this book,
and who also reads a basic text on drugs to start to give them
confidence about working in this area, will be able at least to make
a start on drugs counselling. A good, very brief basic text on drugs
is ISDD's *Drug Abuse Briefing*.

Of course, it is true that most of our drug-using clients will
know a lot more about drugs than we do; but we have to
remember that our clients are not coming to us because we know
about drugs. They will understand that they know more than we
do about drugs: they will often know more about drugs than most
people! And it is important not to pretend that we are expert in
areas where we are not. But in fact most clients who come to us for
help require us to be experts only in how to help people with
problems with drugs to cut down or stop using them. And the
techniques which allow us to help them to do that are contained
in this book.

Second, those of us that work within alcohol-specific agencies
have to be clear that the alcohol problem is the more pressing one,
or the one that the client wants to focus on. If in fact they want to
focus on their drug use, they might be better served by attending
an agency which focuses specifically on drug use. This is not such
an issue, of course, in combined alcohol and drug agencies.

Third, working through the detoxification phase is often more
problematic if someone has problems with both alcohol and other
drugs. If they decide to detoxify from one substance at a time,
they may increase the use of the other substance to compensate for
the loss of effect of the first one. Or if they decide to detoxify from
all their substances at the same time, they may find that this is a
very difficult thing to do, and hence they may relapse more
speedily. Also, the medications used to deal with the effects of
detoxification from various substances at the same time may
interact. For all of these reasons, although (as outlined in Chapter
4) under most circumstances detoxification from alcohol alone is
as effective in an out-patient setting as an in-patient one, with
detoxification from a number of substances, in-patient care might
be a better option.

Alcohol and serious mental health problems

At the same time as there appear to be more people appearing for
help who have both alcohol and other drug problems, there also
appear to be more people who have both alcohol problems and
serious mental health problems. I will explain what I mean by the

term 'serious mental health problems', although it is difficult to do this without recourse to the type of medical/diagnostic language that I do not favour. Nevertheless, there are a number of people whose problems are such that they do not appear to experience reality in the same ways that most of us do – they believe things that most of us do not believe (for example, some people with these problems might believe that other people can control their thoughts) or they see or hear things that we do not see or hear – they suffer from delusions or hallucinations. In psychiatric diagnostic terms, they have psychotic illnesses such as schizophrenia or manic depressive psychosis, where psychosis is defined as 'a mental illness with gross distortion of external reality or with major personality disorganization'.

What should we do as counsellors if someone appears to have a serious mental health problem as well as an alcohol one? In general, we must not try to deal with this sort of problem on our own, and we should refer this person on to a local mental health service. If we have already developed a positive relationship with the client, we might also want to retain our counselling relationship, and continue to work on the alcohol-related issues. If we do this, however, we must be careful to ensure that we keep in close contact with the workers within the mental health services to ensure that we are working in concert, and not at cross-purposes.

If we do work with clients who also have such serious mental health difficulties, we will need to be prepared for a case which might throw up somewhat more problems than usual.

- It may be that such a client is more difficult to engage in our service, or is more difficult to keep engaged in a longer-term relationship if this proves necessary.
- Furthermore, it is very likely that our clients will be prescribed psychoactive medication to deal with their psychotic symptoms, and these again may throw up problems.
- These medications often have negative side-effects which many clients find very distressing, and we may need to provide extra support to help them deal with this without recourse to a return to problematic drinking.
- There may be interactions between alcohol and these medications which may mean that a controlled drinking programme is far less likely to succeed than under less complex circumstances.
- Many counsellors and agencies which support an abstinence model, as well as many AA groups, hold strong views about abstaining from *all* psychoactive substances (although for

some reason they often except nicotine from this view!) and they may find it problematic that these clients are simultaneously giving up some psychoactive substances (alcohol and/or illicit drugs) and at the same time starting to take others (psychoactive medications). Both clients and counsellors have to recognize the differences between substances that are misused and that lead people into major difficulties in life, and substances that are beneficial in reducing highly negative and disadvantageous symptoms which block someone's ability to take their place within mainstream society. It may be useful to role-play with clients how best to counter such views whilst enabling them still to utilize the mutual support that organizations such as AA provide.

Alcohol and depression/anxiety

A third group of clients are those with both alcohol problems and other mental health problems which, although serious and distressing, are not ones which are related to psychotic breakdown. The most common of these other mental health difficulties are anxiety and depression.

Dealing with people who have both alcohol problems and also anxiety or depression is complicated. Anxiety and depression are both common *results* of excessive alcohol consumption, and are also common *triggers* for excessive consumption. Sometimes they are both: a person is anxious or depressed, drinks to relieve these symptoms, finds that alcohol does relieve the symptoms in the short term, and repeats the process, ending up drinking very regularly and/or excessively. Although in the short term alcohol can serve to reduce anxiety and to uplift one's spirits, in the longer term its actions as a central nervous system depressant increases symptoms of both anxiety and depression.

The problem here is which issue to tackle first, or whether or not to tackle the various problems in unison. This of course is the same problem we have examined a number of times already in this book, and is a problem best solved through discussion with the client, taking the lead from them, although informing them of what seems to be a sensible course of action.

It may well be that it would be useful to refer your client to the mental health services, or back to their general practitioner, knowing that these services will be able to offer specific help for both anxiety and depression. Often they will offer psychoactive medication, and anxiety in particular, but also depression, can be greatly helped by some forms of medication.

This, however, raises a number of issues.

First, it is difficult to know whether the anxiety or depression is in fact caused by the excessive alcohol use. It may be that helping the client to deal with his or her alcohol problem means that the other problems lift, once the alcohol ceases to be a problem. It certainly is true that many clients who are displaying symptoms of depression or anxiety at the start of counselling, experience a marked improvement in these symptoms following a few weeks of abstinence. This suggests that it might be best to wait until the effects of a period of abstinence or very reduced drinking have been assessed, before referring on.

On the other hand, we may feel that the decision over when or if to intervene with the anxiety or depression might be better taken by the agency to which we would want to refer. Related to this, there is the difficulty on the part of any prescriber of deciding when to prescribe. Many people with drinking problems are started on antidepressants by their GP before their alcohol problem is fully appreciated. The perceived wisdom is that antidepressants are not any use if people are still drinking, although once people have stopped, it is clear that there will be some who will benefit from an antidepressant. There is also some evidence to suggest that some people might benefit from an antidepressant even if they continue to drink, and hence their depression might be helped even if their alcohol problem is not.

Second, if clients are referred on to other services, and are offered medication, this may cause further problems. There is often a reluctance on the part of many clients to take further drugs, especially at a time when they are seeking our help to stop or reduce their use of substances.

Third, there is the problem outlined above, of agencies or self-help groups taking a strong stand against the use of any psychoactive substance if one is trying to stop using alcohol.

General points relating to all three areas

Similar skills

In summary, when we work with people who have other problems as well as alcohol (be they problems with other drugs, or with their mental health) we use the same skills and techniques that we do when people arrive with ostensibly a 'pure' alcohol problem. There are in fact very few people who only have a problem with alcohol: most have problems in other areas of their lives as well, so in that sense, the people we are discussing in this chapter are no different.

One problem, and one reason why so many people believe that outcomes are often worse when one counsels people with both alcohol and mental health or drug problems, is that it is often more difficult to engage clients with this range of problems in counselling. Again, though, this leads us to look to the skills that we utilize in our everyday counselling of people with alcohol problems, and realize that they are just as applicable here as well. As we have seen throughout Chapters 3 and 4, engaging clients in counselling is a central skill within counselling, and it is being found in the areas of both illicit drug problems and mental health that the motivational interviewing techniques which were originally developed for the alcohol field are extremely useful and effective in these areas as well.

Similar outcomes

There is a general view around that outcomes are often worse with people who have concurrent polydrug or mental health problems. Again, however, this appears to be a myth. One of the few studies which examined this (Project MATCH in the USA) demonstrated that there was not a huge difference between the outcomes obtained, irrespective of people's psychiatric severity. This was especially the case with the Cognitive-Behavioural Therapy (CBT) and the Motivational Enhancement Therapy (MET) arms of the study – clients who had both alcohol and mental health difficulties did fare slightly worse in the 12-Step Facilitation (TSF) intervention.

Particular problems

There are some particular problems which are thrown up when one works with people with the sorts of combined problems that are discussed in this chapter; and in general, such work is more complicated and more difficult than working with alcohol problems alone.

One reason does relate back to the issue of engagement raised above. There is a general problem with mental health work, especially when working with people who possibly have severe problems with all of these areas: alcohol, drugs, serious mental health difficulties, and possibly more common ones as well. It is often very difficult to keep clients with this range of problems adequately engaged with the services. Indeed, that is why the National Service Framework for the Mental Health of Adults of Working Age has insisted that services are developed that are better at engaging and keeping engaged people with these problems. (These services are termed 'assertive outreach' or 'assertive community treatment'.) Such services work with clients with this range of problems to ensure that they continue to keep in therapeutic contact, and continue to take their medication (which is often the major thing that keeps them from being readmitted to a psychiatric hospital). Again, however, ideas of motivational interviewing are being imported into this area to improve engagement, therapeutic relationships, and continued taking of medication.

Another reason relates simply to the complexity of people's problems. It is recognized that this overlap of problems does mean that our clients' difficulties will be potentially harder to solve.

Yet another complication is that clients with both mental health difficulties and drug problems often do find it difficult to see issues clearly. Many of the techniques within this book rely on engaging and interacting with people, and empowering them by that process; and the nature and extent of some of these problems may mean that this empowerment is more difficult to attain.

Conclusion

This is a growing and important area. Using the core skills of counselling outlined in this book, as well as developing some knowledge about the issues to give us confidence in our counselling with these other problems, means that we can be as successful in helping and empowering clients with these problems as we can be with clients who solely have alcohol-related problems.

Key points

- The terms 'dual diagnosis' and 'co-morbidity' imply a medicalized process; they are used here because of their recognizability, and the absence of a meaningful and short alternative.
- Working with people with more than one problem is something that we always do as alcohol counsellors; hence these problems are not very different.
- The numbers of people presenting for help with problems with both alcohol and other drugs are increasing.
- The main difference in working with people with drug as well as alcohol problems is that often we as counsellors need to acquire some basic knowledge of drug problems. This is mainly to give us confidence in working with a new group of people.

- Working through the detoxification phase is more problematic if someone has problems with both alcohol and other drugs, for a variety of reasons. These include the potential to increase one substance as another is detoxed; that relapse may be more common if detox from more than one substance is attempted at the same time; and that the medications used to deal with the effects of detoxification from various substances at the same time may interact. In such cases, in-patient detox might be a better option.
- Work with people with serious mental health problems should be undertaken in collaboration with the local mental health service.
- Such work might throw up special difficulties, including problems with developing or sustaining engagement; client distress over the negative side-effects of strong medication which might increase the chances of a relapse; possible inter-actions between medications and alcohol; and difficulties with a clash of models between abstention from all psychoactive drugs, and the needs of a medication regime.
- Work with more common mental health difficulties can also throw up complications, especially around enabling clients to separate out symptoms which are a result of their alcohol use from symptoms which might have been (and might continue to be) a trigger for their use in the first place.
- Due to this complication, it is difficult to know when to refer on for medical help from either primary care or the secondary mental health services.
- Despite these differences, the similarities with general alcohol counselling work are very strong. When we work with people who have other problems as well as alcohol (whether with other drugs or mental health) we use the same skills and techniques that we do when people arrive with ostensibly a 'pure' alcohol problem.
- Particular problems which do exist when working with clients with this range of problems include engagement, the com-plexity of clients' problems, and the effects of the mental health or drug problems on clients' abilities to see issues clearly within a counselling context.
- Key among the skills we need to use in these cases are our skills of engagement, especially the motivational interviewing techniques, which are increasingly being used in general mental health work because of their effectiveness.
- One myth is that outcomes are often worse with people who have concurrent polydrug or mental health problems. This

appears not to be true: Project MATCH demonstrated that there was no major difference between the outcomes obtained, irrespective of people's psychiatric severity.

References and further reading

Cornwell, A. and Cornwell, V. (1993) *Drugs, Alcohol and Mental Health*. Cambridge: Cambridge University Press.

Gossop, M. (2000) *Living with Drugs*. Aldershot: Ashgate.

Graham, H., Mueser, K., Birchwood, M. and Copello, A. (2001) *Substance Misuse in Psychosis: a Handbook of Approaches to Treatment and Service Delivery*. Chichester: Wiley.

ISDD (1997) *Drug Abuse Briefing*. London: Institute for the Study of Drug Dependence.

Lawson, S. (1995) *Everything Parents Should Know about Drugs*. London: Sheldon Press.

Lee, E. (1997) *Mental Health Care: a Workbook for Carers*. Basingstoke: Macmillan.

McKay, J. and McLellan, T. (1998) 'Deciding where to start: working with polyproblem individuals', in W. Miller and N. Heather (eds), *Treating Addictive Behaviours* (2nd edn). New York: Plenum.

Rorstad, P., Checinski, K., McGeachy, O. and Ward, M. (1996) *Dual Diagnosis: Facing the Challenge*. London: Wynne Howard.

Shaikh, Z. with Reading, J. (1999) *Between Two Cultures: Effective Counselling for Asian People with Mental Health and Addiction Problems*. London: Ethnic Alcohol Counselling in Hounslow (EACH).

Tyler, A. (1988) *Street Drugs: the Facts Explained, the Myths Exploded* (2nd edn). London: Hodder & Stoughton.

---------------------------------- 9 ----------------------------------

Myths and Facts about Problem Drinkers

There are many myths both within society generally and within the alcohol field concerning working therapeutically with problem drinkers. In this chapter I shall deal with some of the more common ones, which often interfere with the counselling work.

'All alcoholics are liars', or 'Alcoholics will always deny their problems'

The idea that those with drinking problems are less likely to tell the truth than other clients is a view held by many people. The ethos of the counselling approach laid out in this book is that people do things for reasons. Therefore, if clients do lie, it must be for a reason. It is the counsellor's job to discover what the reason might be, and to work towards reducing the chances of a client feeling they have to lie.

Do problem drinkers lie more than other people?
I know of no evidence to back up such a statement. Certainly, many people who are well informed about problem drinkers do talk of their lying, but these people are often either family members or counsellors, and, as we shall see, it is not surprising that clients with drinking problems lie to both groups! This, however, is the result of the constraints under which such people put problem drinkers, rather than anything to do with the makeup of the problem drinker.

The whole idea of clients lying is a fundamental denial of a basic counselling stance. The building blocks of counselling are that we listen to a client and work from what they tell us, from their reality – as opposed to starting counselling believing that the client is going to lie to us. The issue here is one of trust: we believe the client's story until contrary evidence (for example, the client contradicting himself) emerges, revealing the need for clarification, challenge and so on, on our part.

Starting with what clients tell us does not mean we believe everything they say is the 'whole truth'. Everyone will reveal only a portion of the truth in the first instance, and even the bit they reveal may not be totally correct – but it is all they are prepared to reveal at that time. This gradual opening up is a process which should not be rushed. Knowing that a client will reveal more as counselling progresses does not mean that what we have learnt so far is untrue.

So, do clients with alcohol-related problems lie more often than other clients? The answer is that they probably do to some people, but if we start off thinking that what the client says is untrue, we have probably lost the client.

If they do lie sometimes or with some people, why?

There are three main reasons for this. The first is that they feel that the consequences of telling the truth would not be in their best interests. For example, in a residential agency where total abstinence is the rule, and where violation will lead to discharge and consequent homelessness, it is not difficult to see why a client would not volunteer this information, and on being challenged with it, would lie. Similarly, in a home environment where admitting to drinking predictably leads to rows and unpleasantness, it is not surprising that the drinker chooses to lie.

The second reason is that clients seek to deny to themselves what they are doing and the consequences of their actions. In this case, the lying is entirely incidental – the client is lying to him/herself, and, therefore, will appear to be lying to everyone else.

So, do clients with alcohol-related problems deny more than clients with other problems? They probably do not deny more than other clients with problem behaviour that is starting to go out of control. Denial, or misattribution, allows people to continue to behave in ways which cause them problems without being forced to acknowledge these problems. To say that people sometimes misattribute events, however, is a far cry from categorizing all problem drinkers as inveterate deniers/liars – this is simply another pejorative term and set of attitudes which people put on to problem drinkers.

The third reason relates to clients' self-esteem: their wish to be seen in the best light by the counsellor, to be a person worth helping. This anxiety may lead to clients revealing only those parts of their behaviour which they think might be acceptable to the counsellor. This may lead to the concealing of drinking – and much other behaviour as well.

If clients do sometimes misattribute the situation, or even sometimes deliberately lie, what should the counsellor do?

First, understand the world from the client's viewpoint. Behaviour is explicable and understandable if we take the time and trouble to try to understand it. Clients do things for reasons, so be prepared to investigate sufficiently to understand what these reasons are.

Second, let the clients know we are going to take this time and trouble. By our words, actions and body language, encourage them to accept that we are interested in them, that we want to engage with them, that we want to help. Help them to realize that not telling us things will in no way harm us – that the person who loses out is the client him or herself, in that inadequate information limits our ability as counsellors.

Third, reassure the client that nothing negative will occur as a result of telling us things. Of course, we cannot guarantee there will never be negative consequences of them giving us information, and it would be inappropriate to suggest to clients that they should treat us as confessors. So sometimes we will have to gently confront a client with the consequences of their actions, and the contract we have built with the client must be one in which both we and the client see this as our role.

'One can't work with someone unless he/she has admitted he/she is an alcoholic'

The issue here revolves around the words 'admit' and 'alcoholic': clients have to 'admit' something, and what they have to admit is that they suffer from the disease of 'alcoholism'.

Clients need to recognize – or to be aware at some level – that a problem exists in order for them to come for help in the first place, but the myth that counsellors cannot start to work therapeutically with clients until the clients admit they are alcoholics has bedevilled the field for many years. This is a myth for a number of reasons.

The first relates to the word 'admit', and raises the question of why we should insist that clients have to admit anything. Having a client attending, and raising the question with us that there might possibly be a problem, or even being willing to think about things, is sufficient for us to be able to start to help. The idea of insisting that clients have to say what we want them to say before we will help them once again transgresses the same basic counselling rule of accepting what the client tells us. The myth here suggests that instead of doing that, we try to force clients to admit something; instead of listening to what they have to say, we try to put words into their mouths.

The second reason again links with the word 'admit', which implies that we are attempting to get clients to agree to something negative and pejorative. The whole idea implies a police inter-rogation, with the counsellor taking the role of policeman, attempting to prise an admission out of the hardened criminal, alibi and all. This model is a far cry from what I understand counselling to be – a warm, caring encounter between someone who at whatever level wants help, and someone who is willing to put time and effort into helping.

Counselling is not about convincing clients. Counselling is about facilitating clients, about empowering them so they can go on to take control over their own lives. A good counsellor does not try to force clients into admitting anything.

Counselling is not about laying down preconditions as to how people describe themselves before the counsellor is prepared to offer help. What a client calls him/herself is immaterial. What is important is that the client acknowledges, at some level, that his/her drinking is related to the problems which have brought him/her to us for help in the first place. If a client recognizes that drinking is related to his/her problems, one can begin to counsel, irrespective of what the client calls him/herself. If he/she does not acknowledge this link, then the job is more difficult. But there is a wide gulf between acknowledging a link between drinking and problems on the one hand, and calling oneself an incurable alcoholic – with all the connotations that includes – on the other.

Terminology is unimportant. It is our job as counsellors to accept the client in whatever terms he or she chooses to present the problem. If clients describe themselves as 'alcoholics', it is not our job to convince them they are not – although we may need to ensure they are not simply transferring responsibility for their behaviour on to 'the disease', which they can blame if they relapse – but if they describe themselves in other terms, this does not need challenging either.

The needless challenging of terminology, and insistence on people describing themselves in uniform ways, has led to large numbers of clients leaving therapy. This has sometimes occurred because clients refused to 'admit' to being alcoholics, which many counsellors take as a sign either of denial, or that the problems are not severe enough to warrant help; and it has also occurred because clients sometimes did 'admit' to alcoholism and hence to a range of problems and a complete model which often did not correspond at all to their perceived reality.

'One can't work with people unless they have reached rock bottom'

The myth that counsellors can only start to work therapeutically with clients when they have reached 'rock bottom' is one of the reasons why counsellors have refused to work with clients whose problems are not too severe. The problems with this idea are manifest: how does one assess when 'rock bottom' is reached? And what sort of counsellor will wish to insist that clients reach the stage of total desperation before they can be accepted as clients?

Fortunately, as with so many ideas drawn from the disease model, this myth is also losing ground: mounting evidence shows that early intervention, long before 'rock bottom' has been reached, is the most effective way of intervening with alcohol problems.

'One can't work with people until they are ready to be helped or admit they have a problem'

There are a number of issues here. The first is the assertion that someone will only change if they want to. In some ways, of course, this is a truism – we cannot force someone to change their behaviour; we have no gun at someone's head, no magic power to alter someone else's wishes. But contained in this is the same oversimplified idea that people are either one thing or another, that they either want to change or they do not.

One of the key ideas introduced in Chapters 3 and 4 was that of ambivalence. Often people come along to a counselling agency wanting help to change, and yet also wanting to continue behaving as they have been. This ambivalence is perfectly normal. The point is that although a person must want to change at some level, by the questions we ask and the way we ask them, we can influence the person over how much he/she wants to change, as opposed to wanting to remain the same.

The second issue implicit in the myth is that one cannot control someone else's behaviour. This is once again both a truism and an oversimplification. It is true that we cannot control someone else's behaviour – except in some cases of legal compulsion – but it is equally true that we can influence the way someone else behaves by the way we behave.

A problem drinker will often come for counselling because of pressure from an employer; or from a spouse; or even from the legal system. Sometimes the person will come purely to keep the peace in the short term, with absolutely no intention of considering any change in behaviour at all. But many others come prepared to listen, and possibly to consider what the counsellor has to say. What then happens is up to the counsellor. The message of Chapters 3 and 4 is that what we do can influence client motivation, and hence behaviour.

The third issue contained within this myth is that people have to admit something in order to be able to be helped, which has been discussed above.

'Abstinence is the only answer to a serious drinking problem'

This is the myth of a single answer. For fifty or more years the disease lobby has argued that the only solution is abstinence, and that anyone who suggested anything different was a charlatan or a rogue. The evidence, however, is overwhelming that some people with very serious alcohol problems do return to some form of moderated drinking. A proportion of these return to controlled drinking, and others seem to be able to return to the less regimented but harm-free form which corresponds more to moderate drinking.

Of course, as we saw in Chapter 4, the fact is that abstaining is an easier activity than controlling one's drinking. Nevertheless, although abstaining is easier, many people still wish to be able to drink in an unproblematic way, and the research shows very conclusively that a minority can do just that.

'There's no point in trying to help "alcoholics" – treatment successes are a real rarity'

As I show in Chapter 4, there is no truth in this myth. Project MATCH (the largest, most statistically powerful and most methodologically rigorous psychotherapy trial ever undertaken in any area, not just with people with alcohol problems), showed that treatment success was the norm, not the exception.

'The only people who can help problem drinkers are those who have an alcohol problem themselves'

It is surprising how many people subscribe to this myth, considering how odd the idea actually is. For example, I have rarely

heard it claimed that in order to help someone with a problem
with schizophrenia, the counsellor needs to have experienced
schizophrenia him or herself. Indeed, imagine the scenario if a
counsellor in the course of one week's work was to see clients
with a variety of problems relating to anxiety, depression, schizophrenia, relationship difficulties, alcohol problems, opiate dependence, and sexual difficulties. It would be worrying if the
counsellor needed to have experienced each of these to be able to
offer effective help.

There is, however, some basis to the idea that in order to
empathize effectively with a client's difficulties, it is useful for us
as counsellors to have had problems of our own at some stage in
our lives. But there is a great deal of difference between having
had some type of problem, and having had the same problem as
the client in front of us. I have argued throughout this book that
helping people deal with their alcohol problems is no different to
helping people deal with any other difficulty. It is important for us
to be able to understand what it means to have a problem, but
there is no reason to suggest that we have to have had the same
problems as our clients.

It is my impression that counsellors who have had drinking
problems themselves are among either the best or the worst of
counsellors. The good ones, while recognizing that everyone's
problems with drinking are different, can selectively utilize their
own experiences to reach a high level of empathy with some of
their clients. The bad ones cannot see further than their own
experiences, and seem to imagine that an analysis of what
happened to them can illuminate all the various events which
clients may bring to share.

The best response to this myth which I have heard is that people
who have almost drowned do not always make the best
swimming instructors.

'But research now shows that alcohol is good for you'

Over the past decade there have been many (sometimes contradictory) reports on the topic of whether drinking some alcohol
might be good for your health. This is an area where new research
is continuing to become available on a regular basis, and it might
be useful to refer to recent evidence at regular intervals. Good
web-sites that might provide this update are the NIAAA in the
USA and Alcohol Concern in the UK (addresses at the end of this
book). Two recently updated NIAAA reports on this topic are
available on the Internet from NIAAA: *Alcohol Alert No. 45* (1999),

and *The 10th Special Report to the US Congress on Alcohol and Health*, especially the section in Chapter 4 on 'Alcohol's effects on the cardiovascular system'. The references for these are: http://silk.nih.gov/silk/niaaa1/publication/aa45.htm   http://silk.nih.gov/silk/niaaa1/publication/10report/10-order.htm.

The research at the moment clearly shows two things. On the one hand, heavy drinking increases the risk of coronary heart disease (CHD), and hence the risk of heart attack. Studies have also shown that binge drinking increases episodes of angina (heart pain) in people with heart disease and raises the risk of fatal heart attack: one study showed that binge drinkers had six times the risk of fatal heart attack compared with moderate drinkers. These studies underline the importance of preventative actions regarding not only the amount of alcohol consumed but also the way people consume it. On the other hand, the research also shows that light to moderate drinking (defined in the USA as one to two drinks per day) is clearly associated with reduced risk of CHD. A key word here is 'associated' – although there is an association between light drinking and reduced risk, it is not certain that the drinking *causes* this reduced risk – it is quite possible that another factor (such as lifestyle, diet or exercise) might be linked with both the light alcohol consumption and the reduced risk.

There is also the issue that, even if alcohol itself is responsible for the lower risk, there is still a trade-off to be considered between these benefits of light drinking, and any risks which might be associated with it. For example, moderate drinking might lower the risk of CHD but might increase the risk of other alcohol-related events such as household accidents, motor accidents, financial difficulties, relationship problems, and so on. As I said in Chapter 1 about sensible drinking guidelines, health issues are only one part of the equation relating to drinking, and other problems can occur at much lower levels of drinking; and people who are pregnant, or on medication, or are very young, or are inexperienced drinkers, or are elderly, may well have far lower limits.

The fact is, however, that as far as our counselling goes, the research summarized above is not really relevant to our clients. Epidemiological data gathered from people who have not developed alcohol problems may well reveal that drinking a small amount of alcohol most days is beneficial in terms of CHD. But our clients in general are people who *have* developed problems with their drinking, and that must be borne in mind when helping them assess what sort of drinking goal they are striving to attain. I discussed in Chapter 4 how I approach the issue of controlled drinking. If clients want to add the evidence of health benefit outlined above to other arguments in favour of attempting control, then we should support them. But this evidence alone is certainly not sufficient for us to be suggesting to clients who are aiming for abstinence that instead they should be seeking to return to drinking; and the same provisos about controlled drinking as I outlined in Chapter 4 still apply – it is a feasible goal for a significant minority, but it is more difficult to achieve, and most people who have had serious problems with their drinking, and who try to control, do not succeed.

Key points

- There are many myths within this area, most of a pejorative kind, which increase the negative way in which people perceive clients with drinking problems.
- Holding the counselling stance stressed within this book makes it difficult to agree with any of these myths: people are individuals who do things for individual reasons; there are reasons for people's behaviour; counselling is a facilitative endeavour which draws out the clients through a process of reflecting, clarifying, challenging, exploring, and so on; these activities are done with, not to, the client.

Relatives of Problem Drinkers

As counsellors who work with alcohol-related problems, we will often be confronted by clients who have alcohol-related problems but who are not themselves drinking. A small number will be clients who have stopped drinking but who need further help – the 'non-drinking drinkers' referred to in Chapter 7. But many others will be family members of problem drinkers.

Relatives of problem drinkers have many problems to contend with. For example, 80 per cent of family violence cases, and at least 20 per cent of child abuse cases, involve alcohol; at least 30 per cent of problem drinkers list marital conflict as a major problem; and 30 per cent of divorce petitions cite alcohol as a contributory factor. It is not surprising that many relatives seek help. Yet often they do not receive it. Why is this?

One of the most difficult tasks is to be confronted by people seeking help because of someone else's drinking. Courses training counsellors to work with problem drinkers often concentrate far more on the drinker than on the family members – and some do not even mention them. This can lead to counsellors feeling de-skilled when they are called upon to deal with the family members; indeed, some agencies seem uncertain whether or not they ought to offer counselling to these people in the first place.

It is the position of this book that these family members – spouses, children, and parents – are legitimate clients both of specialist agencies and of generic helping agencies. Many family members are truly in need of counselling help, and the skills required to work with them are the same as those needed to work with the problem drinkers.

Individual family members

When a family member comes for help, he or she becomes a client in his or her own right. This can raise issues of confidentiality, which were discussed in Chapter 7. What is of paramount importance is to ensure that there is agreement between the client and ourselves as to what the goals of our counselling intervention are. There is nothing worse than us thinking we are helping the client to cope better with the situation, and the client thinking intervention is going to alter the problem drinker's behaviour.

I have often heard people say that we should tell relatives from the outset that we can only help the problem drinker to change if they can persuade the drinker to attend for counselling. *It is my view that this is untrue.* If people behave the way they do partially because the behaviour is rewarded, which then reinforces and maintains that behaviour, then how family members react to the drinker must have an effect. Although it is more difficult to try to change the behaviour of a problem drinker at one stage removed, it is still possible.

What matters are the shared goals of the client, who is the relative, and the counsellor. As with any other client, it is imperative that we are clear as to why he or she has come. The relative may have come simply for information; or for some advice as to how best to deal with the problem drinker; or to try to decide how best to alter the drinker's behaviour; or because the client's relationship with the problem drinker is affected by his or her own problems, which the client now wants to address; and so on.

We should treat these clients in exactly the same way we would treat any other client – with no preconceptions as to why they have come, or what they want to do. The first task, then, is to clarify what this client wants, and how we can help. If he or she wants to attempt to deal with a family member's drinking problem, this is an area where we can help, even if the drinker will not attend in person.

Family members often attend counselling agencies even if they do not immediately declare themselves in a family relationship with a problem drinker. Indeed, it is worrying how often professional helpers such as doctors and social workers do not even ask about drinking, either of the client or of other people, as a possible contributory factor in the genesis of the client's problems.

Common problems

Family members often share a variety of problems. Living with a problem drinker can cause a host of stresses – unpredictability, financial strain, verbal and physical abuse are all more common in the lives of those who live with problem drinkers, be they spouse, child, or parent. It is important that we are aware of these issues when working with a family member on an individual basis.

Some of the tasks we as counsellors might pursue with relatives include:

- listening and helping to reduce anxiety;
- enabling the family member to find out more about alcohol problems and both how they develop and how they can be resolved. Information is power, and family members are like everyone else: the better they understand things, the more in control of events they feel;
- counselling on coping methods – both ways of thinking about the problem, and ways of doing things to alleviate the problem (a number of coping styles are examined below);
- thinking through the range of social support available to the family member, and exploring how best to increase this. It has been shown that being able to talk to others (family, friends, etc.) and being supported by them can greatly reduce the stress of living with a problem drinker;
- referring to appropriate self-help groups;
- helping to improve couple or family communication;
- helping to improve skills concerned with problem-solving.

Numerous issues arise when dealing with a family member:

- Should we try to deal with the current crisis and practical problems which have probably led to the client seeking help at this point – or should we try to deal with the deeper problems of living with a problem drinker?
- Should we try to deal with the person individually, or convene a couple or family session?
- Should we try to do the counselling ourselves, or should we refer on, and if so, to whom?

There are no easy answers to these questions. In the main, I would argue that we must be guided by the client. If he or she wants to be referred on, or only to deal with current concerns, then that is what we should do.

My own preferences would be to deal with both current and deeper problems at the same time, possibly spending a proportion of the session on one issue and a proportion on another; not to refer on, but instead to use other services as sources of advice and support for my own work; and to deal with the problems in the wider context of relationships, as opposed to seeing the problems in isolation, and as individualized in the client.

Coping with a problem drinker is one of the issues with which relatives will often need help. Quite a lot is now known about different ways that family members cope, and how useful or not some forms of coping are. My colleagues and I have grouped ways of coping into three main styles (see Orford et al., 2000). Some people cope by becoming increasingly **engaged with the drinker** (and sometimes with the drinking), and by trying actively to change the drinker's behaviour. Their feelings might be on the one hand: 'There must be something I can do'; or alternatively 'It's not fair on me'. They might demonstrate their engagement by expressing strong emotions to the user, or by starting an argument about the drinking, or by making threats that the relative does not mean to carry out. Alternatively, they might try to control the use of alcohol, by encouraging the drinker to promise not to drink, or by trying to control his or her money in some way; or their engagement might show itself by the family member expressing in a calm and open way their feelings about the drinking and the drinker (although unfortunately, this latter form of engagement is quite rare).

A second style of coping occurs where relatives become very **'tolerant' towards the drinker** and the drinking. Their feelings might be, 'Other people don't understand him/her' or, 'It may be my fault that he/she is drinking' or, 'I would rather have him/her as a drinker than not have him/her at all'. The main contrast with engaged coping is that this way of coping is not a direct attempt to change the alcohol/drug use. In this style of coping, a relative would do things which protect the drinker from the negative consequences of their drinking, such as clearing up mess the drinker has made after he/she has been drinking, making excuses and covering up for the drinker, taking the blame her/himself for the drinker's behaviour, or giving the drinker money even when the relative thinks it would be spent on drink. This way of coping quite often is associated with relatives feeling worried and guilty and they will often feel powerless to change the situation. It is also linked with worse physical and psychological symptoms on the part of the family member.

A third style of coping occurs when family members **withdraw from the drinker** and the drinking. Their feelings may be, 'The less time we spend together the better' or, 'I've got my own life to lead' or, 'I can't help him/her if I go under too'. Withdrawal coping contrasts with both engaged and tolerant coping in that it does not involve attempts to change the drinking in the same way that the engaged coping attempts to; and the family member's actions do not involve protecting the drinker from the negative consequences of the drinking, or joining in with the use of alcohol, in contrast to tolerant coping. In this style of coping, a relative would do things to put physical or psychological distance between themselves and the problem drinker; they may feel a sense of resignation over the problem and feel sad, bitter, and hurt about the situation; or the relative may want to look after her/his own needs, or be developing a feeling of self-reliance. In some ways, this style of coping is similar to Al-Anon's philosophy of 'detach with love', which suggests: 'Look after yourself, but without becoming cold or unloving towards your spouse.'

Clearly there are far more ways of coping than these, but this way of looking at coping has proved very helpful. In summary, the present state of knowledge about coping is that:

- for family members who are adults, 'tolerant' coping seems to be associated with worse outcomes for family members than the other two;
- although withdrawal and avoidance strategies seem to be associated with better outcomes for the family member, they are also linked with worse outcomes for the problem drinker and (if the person withdrawing is the spouse) for the marriage or relationship;
- some forms of engaged coping which are 'anti-drink, not anti-person' can be effective: strategies which suggest being positive to the drinker, while at the same time being negative to the drink – hiding the bottle, throwing away the drink, having a firm rule of 'no drink in the house';
- and confrontation can be a good coping strategy, as long as it is not too aggressive.

Once it is established that we as counsellors should get involved with the family members of people with alcohol problems, it becomes important to clarify the level at which we should be working. Should we be offering counselling, or advice, or information, or support? Should we be involved in setting up support groups for family members? Or should we simply act as transit agencies, referring family members on to self-help groups or other agencies?

It is my view that all of these options will be appropriate for different family members at different times. In the same way that intervention services for problem drinkers are becoming multi-level and pluralistic, with different options being available depending on the needs of the client at the current time, so a wide range of services should be available for the families, to be taken up according to their needs. A network of services is needed to, among other things, assist the family and the user to resist uncontrolled use of alcohol, to mobilize all the resources at the disposal of the family to help with the process of change, and to act at a systemic level within the family.

A further matter concerns the 'not me' issue – many counsellors feel, 'These family members ought to be helped, but not by me'. The reasons given include a need for more specialized knowledge; it is not what the agency is funded for; there are agencies/ counsellors better suited to deal with these problems; and so on. But if we do not help these relatives who need it, then no one will.

Family members who get drawn into counselling

Sometimes we will be pushed into dealing with a family member, having started off trying to help the problem drinker.

People live in a context, both physically and historically. This means that a person's spouse, nuclear and wider family, and the family history, all play a part in the development and maintenance of alcohol-related problems.

This is not to say that spouses or other family members cause the person to develop an alcohol problem: the issue of cause has to be examined on a personal and individual basis. Sometimes family issues are causally connected with the problem drinking, and sometimes they are not. Many people develop their problem over an extended period and for many of them the family/spouse relationship will be the most important relationship during this time of problem development; hence the relationship will be a hugely influential factor both in the problem, and in helping the client deal with it.

Helping the client to change and deal with the drinking will in some relationships lead to major upheavals within the family. For example, people without drinking problems may have taken on roles which were once the drinker's, such as dealing with the finances, paying the bills or disciplining the children, which they might be reluctant to relinquish once the drinker starts to deal with his or her problem. Alternatively, family members may feel bitter or angry towards the drinker, and want him or her to suffer as the family was made to suffer.

These issues mean that frequently it is very difficult to help a client to change his or her drinking and other behaviour without our efforts being undermined by a family member. The solution is often to include them in the counselling sessions, where these issues can be fully dealt with in the open and the change can proceed without undisclosed issues sabotaging the counselling.

Couples and families

Earlier, I suggested that counselling a problem drinker involved two tasks: addressing the problematic drinking *per se*, and dealing with the reasons why the person drank in the past and/or drinks currently. Counselling a couple or a family involves doing the same two things at once. On the one hand, the drinking needs to be addressed; and on the other, the reasons need examining, and alternative strategies need to be developed to enable the drinker to meet whatever needs the drinking fulfils. Working in a couple or family situation means that both aims will be addressed, with all participants present, contributing ideas and discussing practicalities.

Sometimes the problem drinker remains the focus of attention. He or she is the identified 'problem person', and the partner or other family members are there in a quasi-advisory capacity. But often seeing clients in a couple or family context throws up issues and difficulties – many related to the drinking behaviour – which need addressing. Sometimes these issues are sufficiently serious that the counselling cannot succeed unless they are dealt with satisfactorily. In these cases, counselling aimed at helping the couple or family to function more effectively is needed.

This begs the question of whether or not we should do this counselling. Sometimes we might decide not to, and refer the couple/family on to a marriage guidance or local family counselling agency. Sometimes the agency for whom we work might have a clear policy of only seeing clients individually. But there are many reasons why we might not simply refer on, ranging from long waiting lists, to the fact that we have successfully engaged with the couple/family, to the fact that they are asking for us to continue to help.

Common problems

Chapter 7 examines difficult areas and situations in counselling problem drinkers, but there are others which, although overlapping, are specific to couple/family work:

- couples/family members disagreeing;
- couples/family members arguing;
- one partner/member being defensive (one person constantly interrupting with their own version);
- threats to the other partner/member ('If you don't do this, then I'll . . .');

- we as counsellors being pulled in, and colluding or allying with one client against another. There are numerous ways in which we can be sucked in, including being appealed to to decide who is right or wrong in an argument; finding that we like one partner more than the other, or sympathize more with one person than another; finding that we are more attracted to one partner than the other; having one partner put us in the position of being the person who successfully does the things that this person wished his/her partner to do;
- issues concerning confidentiality, if we have seen one of the clients first before seeing them as a couple; or if we are con- currently seeing one client individually.

These concerns and issues are all important, and must be dealt with via the normal supervisory system, and via specific and focused training.

Couple and family counselling is a subject in its own right, and there are many good sources which describe it (see 'References and further reading', p. 183). The rest of this chapter outlines some of the main points concerning couples and family counselling.

Couples counselling (hetero- or homosexual)

There is much in couples counselling that is similar to individual work, and that builds on everything that has so far been dis- cussed. For example, some of the concepts already described which are immensely useful in couples counselling include:

- stages of counselling – trust, exploration, goal-setting, action, maintenance, and ending;
- change as a process;
- our actions as counsellors being dependent on the stage of change reached by the client.

But there are at least three ways in which couples counselling differs:

- it often involves co-work;
- the counsellor does much less talking and much more listen- ing, the main job being to reflect upon and feed back the messages being conveyed;
- the job of the counsellor is to comment on the relationship rather than on the two individuals.

Thus the process of couples counselling is not to intervene individually with two individuals at the same time; instead it is to examine what the interplay of the partners implies about the relationship between them.

While the stages in the process of counselling also apply to couples work, the first stage of developing trust can be far more problematic, for the following reasons.

We may already have begun seeing one person before considering couples counselling. This could lead to problems with either partner – with the new one because he or she might feel we are siding with the person with whom we already have a relationship, and with the existing one because he or she might fear that the close relationship with 'his' or 'her' therapist will be broken, or that something might be said which could show up the story that he or she has told in a different light.

Sexual issues will arise. We may be placed in the 'paragon of virtue' role by the opposite-sex partner, with the implicit – or even explicit – message to the partner of the same sex as us that 'If only you (the partner) could be like "x" (the counsellor), life would be wonderful'; or we may be accused explicitly or implicitly of conspiring with the same-sex client to form an alliance against the other sex partner: 'It's just like men (or women) to stick together.'

Once couples counselling has started, many other issues may arise, such as rivalry for our interest and attention, jealousy, competition, exclusion.

We may have difficulties in developing trust when we are immersed in trying to relate to two, possibly arguing, people at the same time, often in the face of one or both partners attempting to form an exclusive dyadic relationship with us, while we are trying to relate to them as a couple.

These difficulties in creating trust and in forming a working alliance with both participants are not described in order to deter us from attempting couples counselling. They are meant to put us on our guard against common problems, so that we can take evasive action; this might include:

- openly discussing the ways in which our previous relationship with one of the couple might complicate matters, and suggesting solutions;
- addressing the couple jointly rather than individually;
- balancing the attention given so that both have equal amounts (although what might be good for one partner might be too little for the other);
- having a co-worker of the opposite sex who is new to the couple. This can ensure that sex issues are balanced, and that the other issues are not allowed to dominate the counselling.

Once trust is established, there are a number of major areas which are commonly addressed in couples counselling. These include:

- communication – Here it is important to ensure that couples devote sufficient time to communicating, and have the skills to do so. Couples may communicate, but in ways which do not match the needs of the other partner: 'You never say you love me!' 'But I give you flowers!'
- empathy – Many couples, although they do communicate, cannot see the world from each other's perspective. They lack the ability to see the world from another's viewpoint.
- secrets – These may be secrets shared within the relationship but not outside, or they may be secrets which one partner feels must be kept from the other.
- sex – Issues here include sexual difficulties, and one or both partners having or having had affairs.
- goals – Both generally in life, and currently within the relationship.
- changes – This links in with other historical issues, both within the relationship and before: why did they choose each other? Are there intergenerational continuities at work?

Related to these areas are: differences in the model of a relationship which each party may have, for example from believing it is best to do everything together, to believing it is important to do lots of things apart; equality issues, where the type of relationship one partner wants is very different to the one wanted by the other partner; and 'breach of contract' issues, where one party (or both parties) thinks the other has breached the agreed contract.

All these issues can be summed up by asserting that a good relationship requires four components – the four Cs:

- Contract – Both parties need to be clear about what they want from a relationship, and that their partner wants the same things.
- Contact – In order for a relationship to work the partners need to spend time together.
- Communication – The partners need to discuss and share their evaluations of how their aims about the relationship are being met.
- Commitment – The partners need to be committed to making their relationship work, and hence to undertaking the other three components.

Steps in couples counselling

There are a variety of tasks that a counsellor working with a couple ought to pursue. The first of them – listen to their concerns – is identical to the first task of individual counselling, but thereafter they differ:

- Get them to talk to each other, not to us.
- Get them to listen to each other.
- Clarify that there are communication difficulties, and why these exist.
- Reformulate or reframe.

This last point requires clarification.

The two clients will often present two different perspectives, and it is our job to reformulate these in one of two ways. First, we might try to show that the two views are different angles on the same cycle of events. Schroder (1989: 64) gives a good example:

> A husband . . . might claim that trouble always starts when his wife takes to going out at night. As a result, he becomes concerned, starts questioning her when she comes home, but is met with what he feels to be indifference. He therefore takes issue with her when she plans to go out next, and, in the face of her reluctance to listen, is moved to make his point more forcefully. Rather than considering his wishes, she absents herself even more frequently and a major row which has been building over weeks finally erupts. If only she would show more consideration, none of this need ever happen.
>
> His wife for her part might say that things go quite smoothly until her husband has one of his jealous turns. He then starts persecuting her with unreasonable questions, and generally makes the atmosphere at home so miserable that she goes out to let him simmer down. However, far from becoming calmer, he seems to positively take pleasure in getting at her, and, try as she may to get out of his way to avoid a row, it finally erupts. If only he could get a grip on himself none of this need ever happen.

Second, as Schroder comments, problems often arise from natural stresses which occur at different stages in the life cycle. For example, both partners in the couple may have to cope with setting up house, having a first (and subsequent) baby, adolescent children, ailing parents, children leaving home, retirement – all of which require adjustment from both partners. Furthermore, this list mentions only *predictable* life crises; there will also be unexpected changes which can have the same effect. Enabling the couple to reformulate these events as a 'normal' life crisis normalizes the distress they feel, and reduces their feelings of guilt.

One of our central tasks as counsellors is to engage the client, to ensure that he or she will return. This is equally true in couples counselling, although it is correspondingly more difficult, due to the necessity of engaging both partners. Some of the techniques I have found useful with couples generally (as well as when one member has an alcohol problem) are outlined below.

ANALYSE THEIR TIME TOGETHER   The tasks here are first, to clarify whether or not they are spending sufficient time in contact with each other to allow the possibility of a minimum of sharing of activities or communication to occur; second, to clarify whether or not there are spaces in this time spent together which are long enough to be able to communicate satisfactorily; and third, if these are not occurring, to pinpoint why these necessary contact and communication activities are absent. For example, are there repeat patterns, failures to negotiate, failures to express what is wanted, lack of shared interests and activities? (In the first instance, I often ask clients to do this as a homework task.)

WORK OUT WAYS OF INCREASING REWARDING ACTIVITIES TOGETHER, THE POSITIVE ELEMENTS BETWEEN THEM, AND TRUST   Often clients do not realize that even simple things such as giving flowers, a kiss, a compliment, or a special meal are important currency that improves relationships disproportionately to the effort expended.

TRAIN THEM IN NEGOTIATING, PROBLEM-SOLVING, AND COMMUNICA-TING   This needs to include the working concepts of exchange, flexibility, and contracts; and the communication skills of listening, non-interruption, reflection, and so on. It is often necessary also to help the clients to clarify the differences between assertion and aggression, and between negotiation and confrontation. For example, 'You never take my feelings into account, and I'm not going to stand for it any longer' is a confrontational approach which often sabotages any attempt at negotiation.

A useful technique which can enable a client to begin to see the world from his or her partner's perspective is to ask the clients to reverse roles. This could be in the session, with one acting out what he or she thinks the other would say or do in response to a given comment or action; or outside of the session, where one partner might perform the roles and tasks commonly performed by the other.

ENCOURAGE THEM TO ENGAGE IN 'BONDING' ACTIVITIES   Because many clients become relatively estranged from one another, it is important for them to do more things together, talking more, disclosing more.

HELP TO REASSESS THE RELATIONSHIP   Many clients have unrealistic expectations of what a relationship involves. For example, many are surprised that a relationship needs open communication. One recent client voiced a familiar refrain when she said she believed it was wrong to need to make things explicit: 'In an ideal marriage, people should know what their partner is thinking without needing to talk'!

Clients in couples counselling have to be introduced gradually to the notion of being specific about their needs, as opposed to believing their partner should mystically 'know' without being told. As they begin to accept that communication is necessary, they often need to be helped to make the communications explicit and specific: 'You never take my feelings into account', a general complaint, is very different from 'I need to feel an equal part of this relationship; please will you consult me before doing things which commit both of us to doing something', which is far more specific, and suggests action the other partner can implement.

Other examples of unrealistic expectations might be couples who do not realize that conflict is inevitable in a relationship; that an argument does not imply the failure of the relationship; or that relationships pass through good and bad patches, rather than remaining at a high or even moderately tolerable level. Many clients need to gain an understanding that relationships evolve and change. They need to learn that if one wants a relationship to last, the task is to try to ensure that the evolution is in a direction which is desired by, or at least acceptable to, both partners.

FURTHER HOMEWORK TASKS   I have found the following useful to focus clients' minds during couples counselling. Each partner is asked separately to answer questions such as:

- 'Where do I see myself in (say) two years' time?'
- 'Where do I see our relationship in (say) two years' time?'
- 'Where would I like our relationship to get to in "x" years' time?'

Answers are fed back to the other partner in the sessions, and assessed for their degree of realism, and the extent to which they improve on the four Cs – contract, contact, communication, and commitment.

This brief examination of couples counselling merely sets the scene. Couples work is tremendously interesting and challenging, and is certainly not something counsellors should shy away from, but it might be a good idea for us to attend a training day or two, or work with a more experienced couples counsellor before attempting to take on couples on our own.

Finally, sometimes the wording of this section has assumed a heterosexual couple relationship, but everything I have said applies equally well to single-sex relationships.

Family counselling

Family counselling is both very similar and very different to couples counselling. It is similar in that the focus of attention is not the individual client but the set of relationships between those attending. The counsellor seeks to help the clients to reflect upon their interactions and change their behaviour within the family context. It is different in that there are more people participating – which makes it more difficult to see the major lines of the session developing – and because it is a much more varied field theoretically, with a huge variety of terms and ideas introduced, which have had major influences on counselling and family therapy. For example:

- communication patterns and the 'double-bind' (Bateson, 1973);
- family in homoeostasis (Jackson, 1965);
- boundary issues and enmeshment (Minuchin and Fishman, 1981);
- cross-generational coalitions (Hayley, 1976);
- family myths (Byng-Hall, 1973);
- invisible loyalties and alliances (Boszormeni-Nagy and Spark, 1973);
- secrets in the family (Pincus and Dare, 1978).

These ideas often seem rather esoteric unless one becomes steeped in family therapy ways of thinking. A more useful way may be to consider the following when seeing a family.

FAMILY STRUCTURE   The way a family is structured often provides a useful insight into both how problems may have evolved and how they might be tackled. Family structure can include such issues as who has the power; who does what (for example who deals with finance, discipline); what are the age and sex boundaries (for example who is allowed in the bathroom with whom).

FAMILY PROCESSES   How does the family conduct itself? Where are the alliances? Where is the hostility – at which individual or set of individuals, or at which alliance, is it directed? Families usually have a state to which they return if events knock them off balance, which is known as 'homoeostasis'.

FAMILY HISTORY   The individuals within the family, and the family as an entity, will have a history, which can provide insight into the problems. For example, is there a history of problem drinking, or other excessive behaviour, in either side of the family? If there is – with one of the parents, for example – how did the family react to that at the time, and is this influencing how the family is reacting to the current problem?

FAMILY PATTERNS OF COMMUNICATION   Families often have typical ways of communicating. Who talks to whom, about what, and when? Who keeps secrets from whom? Who has alliances with whom and about what?

FAMILY FUNCTIONING   The family does some things easily and others with difficulty. What are these things, and how can they be used to develop an intervention strategy to help the family?

FAMILY LIFE CYCLE   The family will be at a particular period in its life cycle. For example, a baby may have recently been born, or children may have left home, or a parent may have died. How has this affected the problem, and why has the family presented for help at this point?

FAMILY CRISIS   As counsellors we often meet a family at a time of crisis – for example when some members have left or are about to leave home. How has this crisis affected the family, and why has it led to them presenting for help at this time?

When working with a family, some of the above might prove useful, along with some of the issues raised below.

Try to understand how the family works. This is best done by a mixture of asking questions relating to the issues above, and simply observing how the members respond and react towards each other.

We can ask questions in a variety of ways. One is to ask for explanations of differences, for example:

- between people – 'Who gets more upset when "x" happens, Mum or Dad?'
- between relationships – 'Is your wife closer to Gavin or Tracey?'
- between perceptions or beliefs – 'When people cry, is it to get their own way, or because they are in pain?'
- between actions and events – 'What would be most comforting: to leave him alone, or to comfort him?'
- between time periods – 'Is there more fighting now than before your mother's stroke?'

All these questions can help to elicit an understanding of the alliances and other family processes and structures, which can give a picture of the problematic issues.

Try to facilitate change. Due to the process of homoeostasis, families have proved to be notoriously resistant to change; yet by intervening at the family level we are utilizing a model which suggests that the family needs to change to enable the individuals within it to alter their behaviour.

Among the techniques we might use to try to encourage a family to develop new ways of functioning are: reframing, and reflexive circular questioning. Reframing enables clients to see the situation in a different, and hopefully more positive, way. Examples might include: 'Helen is really trying to keep you all together when she does these things'; and, 'Your arguments certainly tell me how much you all care about each other, because you care enough to argue, as opposed to simply being indifferent to each other.' Besides facilitating change in the ways family members perceive each other, these interventions create pauses in the repetitive cycle the family has built up, and that pause can be used by us and by the family to alter feelings and responses.

With reflexive circular questioning, questions are used to trigger off a change and to off-balance participants, rather than to explore issues. An example might be for us, in the middle of an argument between parents in an interview, to ask the child, 'When your parents argue at home, is it more or less intense than it is here and now?'

Other ways of helping the family to move on use ideas which are similar to those discussed in previous chapters, and those mentioned earlier in this chapter in couples counselling. These include goal-setting, and empowering clients to carry out new behaviour; and clarifying communication between participants.

Children of problem drinkers

Many clients with drinking problems strongly contend that their drinking has not affected their children; some even argue that their children do not know of the drinking at all. In almost all cases, *this is not true*. There are many children of problem drinkers, and almost all of them both know about and are affected by their parents' drinking. It was estimated in 1985 that one in every eight Americans is the child of a problem drinker, which makes over six million young people under the age of 18, and 22 million adults over 18 in the US.

Interviews with children of problem drinkers reveal they know all too well about their parents' drinking. They report that the parent acts 'oddly', which may mean they are violent, argumentative, or aggressive; or they are withdrawn; or they get very drunk and show the family up; or they disrupt family occasions. In families where only one parent has the drinking problem, the children also talk about how 'oddly' the other parent acts: this parent may start to drink excessively as well, or take on roles which used to be the drinking parent's. The other parent may also put all their attention on to their drinking spouse and ignore the child; or they may become negative towards their drinking spouse.

All these things lead to reactions from children. They develop problems such as withdrawal, crying, or illnesses; or aggression, delinquency, and drug or alcohol abuse. Their academic performance may deteriorate, their self-esteem may diminish. Research into the children of problem drinkers has shown that they have more of all of these problems than do other children. A consistent picture has emerged that parental alcohol problems lead to a high risk of such children developing difficulties in four areas:

- anti-social behaviour and conduct disorder – delinquency, truancy, aggressive behaviour, hyperactivity, temper tantrums;
- school environment problems – learning difficulties, reading retardation, conduct and aggressive behaviour, poor school performance, general loss of concentration;
- emotional – general emotionally disturbed behaviour, negative attitudes towards the problem-drinking parent, or towards the parents' marriage as a whole, psychosomatic complaints, self-blame;

- adolescence – division between peer relationships and home life; social isolation, attention-seeking behaviour, leaving home early, early use of alcohol and other drugs.

A parent with a drinking problem causes all sorts of havoc within a family: the problem disrupts the cohesion of the parental and the family relationships, or one or both parents may emotionally withdraw from the child. The child may respond in a variety of ways, probably leading to lowered self-esteem, anxiety, emotional detachment, perceived isolation, and so on. They may also develop ambivalent and conflicting attitudes to alcohol – negative because it causes so many problems, yet positive because parents have modelled the use of alcohol as a way of coping with problems, albeit a not very effective one.

Why are children affected?

Children have a variety of needs that must be fulfilled. They need love, affection, and nurturance – but they also need a clear structure. Parental alcohol problems often lead to children not getting any of these needs met – because of separation, the loss of a parent if all contact is broken when the couple part, or the problems between the couple even if they do not part.

Much research has demonstrated that important issues which help determine whether or not children are affected include: violence, even if it is not directed at the child; marital conflict, which is in fact the major concern of the children; separation, divorce, and parental loss; and inconsistency and ambivalence in parenting. All these lead to unpredictability, which can lead in turn to deteriorating parent/child relationships, diminishing self-esteem on the part of the child, increasing social isolation, and increasing feelings of exclusion.

The same body of research has shown that there are factors which can protect children from this harm, including the other parent, and whether or not he or she provides sufficient positive attention; other important people, such as a teacher or a grand-parent; or a cohesive parental or family relationship despite the problem drinking. These are all factors which lead to attachment and security, which leads on to an ability to relate to others later in life.

What can we do about the children?

There are a number of clear implications for us as counsellors. The first is that the children of clients with alcohol problems need help. Their involvement with somebody who can offer counselling is crucial. The second is that we cannot simply hope that this help will be offered by someone else. For example, most children do not refer themselves for help; they are referred, usually by a parent. The parents in this case are unlikely to refer their children, particularly if they are desperate to believe that the drinking and other problems are having no effect on their children. So the people who are best able to help, either directly or by referring on, are we, the counsellors, who have started to develop a relationship with the problem drinker or with other relatives. We are the people most likely to be aware of children who need help. It is up to us to ensure that services exist to which these children can be referred.

One thing we could do might be to involve the children in our counselling. Instead of offering couples counselling, we could offer family work. Alternatively, we could offer the children sessions, either with ourselves, or with colleagues. We might pursue similar tasks with a child as with any other relative: listening and helping to reduce anxiety; counselling them concerning coping methods; helping them to improve skills concerned with problem-solving; and referring them to appropriate self-help groups.

Conclusion

Relatives of problem drinkers are often badly affected by the problem drinker and need help. As counsellors who understand something about problem drinking, we are well placed to offer informed help to these relatives. If we do not, the chances are that no one else will. We might see relatives individually, or with the problem drinker as a couple, or within their family. There are skills and techniques which are useful at all levels, but the basic counselling processes remain the same.

Key points

- Relatives of problem drinkers have many problems to contend with. It is not surprising that many relatives seek help, yet often they do not receive it. These family members (particularly spouses, children, and parents) are legitimate clients both of specialist agencies and of generic helping agencies.
- Courses training counsellors to work with problem drinkers concentrate far more on the drinker than on the family members. This often leads to counsellors feeling de-skilled

when they are called upon to deal with the family members. Yet the skills needed to work with them are the same as those needed to work with the problem drinkers.

- Frequently it is difficult to help a client to change his or her drinking and other behaviour without our efforts being undermined accidentally or deliberately by a family member. The solution is often to include them in the counselling.

- Family members often need help in their own right. This help will often involve listening and reassuring them, enabling them to acquire further information about alcohol and alcohol problems, exploring how they are coping and whether they have thought about alternatives, and enabling them to utilize social support from as many sources as possible.

- Often seeing clients in their couple or family context throws up issues and difficulties which need addressing. Sometimes we might feel these issues are so serious that the counselling cannot succeed unless these couple/family difficulties are dealt with satisfactorily.

- There are problematic areas and situations specific to couples/family work. These include couples/family members disagreeing or arguing; one partner/member being very defensive; threats to the other partner/member; ourselves as counsellors being pulled in, and colluding or allying with one client against another; particular issues concerning confidentiality, if we have seen one of the clients first before seeing them as a couple, or if we are concurrently seeing one client individually. These concerns and issues are all important, and must be dealt with via both the normal supervisory system, and via specific and focused training.

- There is much in couples counselling which is similar to individual work, and which builds on everything discussed in this book. But there are at least three ways in which couples counselling does differ: it often involves co-work; the counsellor does much less talking and much more listening, with the main job being to reflect upon and feed back what appear to be the messages being conveyed; and the job of the counsellor is to comment on the relationship rather than on the individuals.

- Engaging couples in counselling is difficult, due to the necessity of engaging both partners. There are a variety of techniques I have found useful with couples.

- Family counselling is different to couples counselling in that there are more people participating, which makes it relatively more complex and difficult to see the major lines of the session developing; and because it is theoretically a much more varied field.

- Many clients with drinking problems strongly contend that their drinking has not affected their children. Some even argue that their children do not know of the drinking at all. In almost all cases, this is not true. There are a great many children of problem drinkers, and almost all of them both know about, and are affected by, their parents' drinking.

References and further reading

Couples and family counselling

Barker, P. (1998) *Basic Family Therapy*. Oxford: Blackwell Science.

Bateson, G. (1973) *Steps to an Ecology of Mind*. St Albans: Paladin.

Boszormeni-Nagy, I. and Spark, G. (1973) *Invisible Loyalties*. New York: Harper & Row.

Butler, C. and Joyce, V. (1997) *Counselling Couples in Relationships*. Chichester: Wiley.

Byng-Hall, J. (1973) 'Family myths used as a defence in conjoint family therapy', *British Journal of Medical Psychology*, 131: 433–47.

Carpenter, J. and Treacher, A. (1989) *Problems and Solutions in Marital and Family Therapy*. Oxford: Blackwell.

Carpenter, J. and Treacher, A. (eds) (1993) *Using Family Therapy in the Nineties*. Oxford: Blackwell.

Carr, A. (1995) *Positive Practice: a Step-by-step Guide to Family Therapy*. Chur, Switzerland: Harwood.

Carr, A. (2000) *Family Therapy: Concepts, Process and Practice*. Chichester: Wiley.

Dryden, W. (ed.) (1985) *Marital Therapy in Britain, Vols 1 and 2*. London: Harper & Row.

Freeman, D. (1990) *Couples in Conflict*. Milton Keynes: Open University Press.

Gilbert, M. and Shmukler, D. (1996) *Brief Therapy with Couples*. Chichester: Wiley.

Hayley, J. (1976) *Problem-Solving Therapy*. San Francisco: Jossey-Bass.

Jackson, D. (1965) 'The study of the family', *Family Process*, 4: 1–20.

Lee, E. (1997) *Mental Health Care: a Workbook for Carers*. Basingstoke: Macmillan.

Minuchin, S. and Fishman, H. (1981) *Techniques of Family Therapy*. Cambridge, MA: Harvard University Press.

Noon, M. (1999) *Counselling and Helping Carers*. Leicester: BPS Books.

Pincus, L. and Dare, C. (1978) *Secrets in the Family*. London: Faber & Faber.

Reimers, S. and Treacher, A. (1995) *Introducing User-Friendly Family Therapy*. London: Routledge.

Schroder, T. (1989) 'Couple counselling', in W. Dryden, D. Charles-Edwards and R. Woolfe (eds), *Handbook of Counselling in Britain*. London: Routledge.

Stogdon, M. (1995) *Working with Men in Family Therapy*. Norwich: Social Work Monographs.

Stow, J. (1994) *Sexual Abuse, Feminism and Family Therapy*. Norwich: Social Work Monographs.

Street, E. (1989) 'Family counselling', in W. Dryden, D. Charles-Edwards and R. Woolfe (eds), *Handbook of Counselling in Britain*. London: Routledge.

Street, E. and Dryden, W. (1988) *Family Therapy in Britain*. Milton Keynes: Open University Press.

Family members of problem drinkers

Barber, J. and Crisp, B. (1995) 'The "Pressures to Change" approach to working with the partners of heavy drinkers', *Addiction*, 90: 269–76.

Collins, R.L., Leonard, K. and Searles, J. (eds) (1990) *Alcohol and the Family*. New York: Guilford.

Copello, A., Orford, J. Velleman, R., Templeton, L. and Krishnan, M. (2000) 'Methods for reducing alcohol and drug related family harm in non-specialist settings', *Journal of Mental Health*, 9: 329–43.

Meyer, M. (1982) *Drinking Problems = Family Problems*. Lancaster: Momenta.

Meyers, R. and Smith, J. (1995) *Clinical Guide to Alcohol Treatment: The Community Reinforcement Approach*. New York: Guilford.

Meyers, R., Smith, J. and Miller, E. (1998) 'Working through the concerned significant other', in W. Miller and N. Heather (eds), *Treating Addictive Behaviours* (2nd edn). New York: Plenum.

O'Farrell, T. (ed.) (1993) *Treating Alcohol Problems: Marital and Family Interventions*. New York: Guilford Press.

Orford, J. et al. (2001) 'Tolerant-inaction is bad for your health: data from relatives coping with drug and alcohol problems in Mexico City and South West England', *Addiction*, in press.

Paolino, T. and McCready, B. (1977) *The Alcoholic Marriage. Alternative Perspectives*. New York: Grune & Stratton.

Seixas, J. (1979) *How to Cope with an Alcoholic Parent*. Edinburgh: Canongate.

Velleman, R. (1996) 'Alcohol and drug problems: an overview of the impact on children and the implications for practice', in M. Gopfert, J. Webster and M. Seeman (eds), *Seriously Disturbed and Mentally Ill Parents and their Children*. Cambridge: Cambridge University Press.

Velleman, R. (2000) 'Alcohol and the family', in D. Cooper (ed.), *Alcohol Use: The Handbook*. Abingdon: Radcliffe Medical Press.

Velleman, R. and Orford, J. (1999) *Risk & Resilience: Adults Who Were the Children of Problem Drinkers*. London: Harwood.

Velleman, R., Copello, A. and Maslin, J. (eds) (1998) *Living with Drink: Women Who Live with Problem Drinkers*. London: Longman.

Ward, M. (1998) *Caring for Someone with an Alcohol Problem*. London: Age Concern.

11

Summary

I s it possible to sum up an entire book in a few selected phrases? This last brief chapter will attempt to do exactly that.

The book argues that:

- clients are deeply individual; in order to help them, we need to work on an individual level.
- we use the same skills with problem drinkers that we use in counselling any person with any problem. People drink problematically for reasons. Working with alcohol-misusing clients means we need to deal simultaneously with their alcohol use and their other difficulties.
- in assessing a client's alcohol problems, we should examine the client's alcohol use; the drinking behaviour; the effects of the use of alcohol; the client's thinking concerning the alcohol use (expectations, values, definition of the problem, understanding of its cause); and the context (family, employment, social) within which the client has been drinking.
- counselling the client with drinking problems requires the same skills as counselling any other problem. We need to develop trust, explore the problem, help to set goals, empower clients to take action, help them to maintain changes, and agree when the time comes to end our counselling relationship. In counselling, we are responsible for the process; the main responsibility for the content lies with the client.
- there are also techniques which are especially relevant to problem drinkers: giving clients information and simple advice as to how to cut down or give up; helping the client to set intermediate, short-term goals which are (and seem to the client to be) achievable; helping problem drinkers to become more aware of the forces within their environments which push them towards drinking; using more active techniques to help them to rethink what they can do.

- controlled drinking goals are legitimate ones for clients to aim towards if the client wishes to, although controlled drinking is more difficult than abstaining.
- if we think clients are aiming for the wrong goal, we should tell them we are happy to back them up but that personally we think they have chosen incorrectly, and why we think this.
- clients need to know that even if they do relapse, we want them to return and discuss the situation with us.
- relapse management is like the other parts of counselling: understanding the reasons for a client's behaviour; understanding the central role a client's expectations and beliefs play in determining his or her behaviour; and enabling a client to learn new, and utilize already learnt, skills.
- it is possible to offer help to clients with drinking problems in groups, although there is a range of reasons both for and against such help.
- helping clients who have other serious problems as well as their alcohol use is also possible, although it may be more difficult.
- there are many myths which increase the negative way in which people perceive working with clients with drinking problems. However, holding the counselling stance stressed within this book makes it very difficult to agree with any of these myths, since:

  - people are individuals who do things for individual reasons;
  - there *are* reasons for people's behaviour;
  - counselling draws out the client through a process of reflecting, clarifying, challenging, exploring;
  - these activities are done with, not to, the client;
  - alcohol use lies along a continuum: there is no simple dividing line between 'alcoholic' drinkers and the rest of the population;
  - individuals can move along this continuum in either direction;
  - individuals learn how to behave towards alcohol, and this is open to change;
  - if people continue to use alcohol despite developing problems, this must occur for reasons.

- relatives of problem drinkers have many problems to contend with. It is not surprising that many seek help, yet often they do not receive it.

It has been my experience that using the principles summarized above is the best way of helping people with drinking problems.

Appendix 1
Facilities in the UK providing help for people with alcohol problems

Volunteer responses

Most 'voluntary agencies' are in fact not voluntary at all – see below under 'Grant-supported voluntary facilities'. Nevertheless, there are a few which do not accept any financial reward for their work.

Alcoholics Anonymous (AA). This is an international self-help organization. People who *have had* a serious drinking problem provide a voluntary, self-help service to those who *currently have* a serious drinking problem. AA subscribes heavily to the disease concept of alcoholism, defines its members as alcoholics, and insists that the cause of alcoholism lies only within the alcoholic. It is based on a belief that the only solution to 'alcoholism' is total and lifelong abstinence, and it utilizes the '12-step' approach, which it invented. This approach uses 12 statements which participants need to work through and come to believe. The first one is 'We admitted we were powerless over alcohol – that our lives had become unmanageable', with the second one being 'We came to believe that a Power greater than ourselves can restore us to sanity.'

Al-Anon. This is almost a mirror image of AA, except that it exists to help support the families of 'alcoholics'. Hence it is an international self-help organization, holding a clear disease concept of 'alcoholism'. As with AA, it is run voluntarily by people who have been through similar experiences to those of the people they are trying to help.

Al-Ateen. This is for teenage children of 'alcoholic' parents.

Volunteer counsellors. These are usually trained members of the general public who volunteer their time. Volunteer counsellors might work in any of the agencies listed in the following sections, but the most common scenario in Great Britain is for them to work in alcohol advisory centres or other local agencies, and to be accredited under the national Volunteer Alcohol Counsellor Training Scheme (VACTS) programme, administered by Alcohol Concern in England and Wales and the Scottish Council on Alcohol in Scotland. It is likely that the VACTS programme will change over the next few years, but it is uncertain what it will develop into. Options include:

- the rolling out of the QuADS [Quality in Alcohol and Drug Services] organizational standards and competencies which have been widely consulted upon in
  the recent past;
- the development of National Occupational Standards for those in the substance
  misuse sector, on which National Vocational Qualifications (NVQs) would be
  based;
- or asking the proposed National Treatment Agency to have a remit for the
  development and maintenance of standards in services, and to include both
  QuADS standards, and some sort of accreditation role for all agency activity
  (including both individual competency accreditation, and the accreditation of
  organizational practice standards, which are a major part of the VACTS
  programme).

At the time of writing (autumn 2000), no final decisions have been made on
which of these routes any VACTS replacement scheme will take.

Samaritans and other volunteer organizations. These include MIND, RELATE, CRUSE,
Age Concern, and so on. People experiencing alcohol problems may contact these
organizations, instead of or as well as the specialist helping agencies.

Grant-supported voluntary facilities

These agencies confusingly often go under the name of 'voluntary agencies' or the
'voluntary sector', although they are rarely run on a voluntary basis. They employ
staff in much the same way, and often on the same salary scales, as do statutory
agencies, but they are usually registered charities, run by management committees,
and they usually receive their funding as grants from either statutory authorities or
from other charities.

Alcohol advisory centres and/or local councils on alcohol/alcoholism. These offer advice,
counselling, and information, and often refer on to health or other services if
necessary. Many use an open-access system, but some operate on an appointment
basis only. They usually operate from an accessible base near a city/town centre.
Many agencies utilize trained volunteers to do some or all of the counselling;
others use only paid staff. Some agencies also offer similar help to those with drug-
related problems.

Hostels. Residential accommodation with a commitment to alcohol therapy. Often
run by a Local Council on Alcohol, or a housing association.

Other organizations. Cyrenians, night shelters. These agencies are concerned with
homelessness and 'down-and-out' problems, so they come into frequent contact
with people with alcohol problems.

(Many of these organizations also operate 'outreach' work, providing services
within the premises of other agencies, such as primary care or probation.)

Statutory facilities

These are usually health-authority or joint health and local authority funded. Each
National Health Service region and each district health authority has slightly

different facilities for alcohol misusers. As with the grant-supported agencies, many of these statutory organizations also operate 'outreach' work, providing services within the premises of other agencies, such as primary care or probation.

Detoxification. Most psychiatric hospitals and some general hospitals provide some bed space for those who need in-patient care under medical supervision while reducing or stopping their alcohol intake. Increasingly, however, detoxification is undertaken on an out-patient basis.

Detoxification units. These are specialized units where trained staff deal with medical, psychological, and social aspects of detoxification. They also provide specialist help as an alternative to imprisonment for those clients who repeatedly come before the courts on alcohol-related charges. There are many examples of such centres which have been attempted in the US and Canada. In the UK, the Department of Health and Social Security set up two types on an experimental basis, one being medical in that it was attached to a general hospital and run by doctors; the other being social in that it was based in the community and run by social workers. In both cases the police were the main referral agents.

Alcoholism treatment units (ATUs). It used to be regional NHS policy to have an ATU in each region, but they have now been largely phased out in favour of community facilities. An ATU is an in-patient unit, usually based within a psychiatric hospital, offering groupwork, counselling, withdrawal from alcohol, withdrawal relief, and so on. They usually have a large AA connection, using both the basic AA ideas (such as the '12-step' approach), and having AA members come into the unit to run AA groups.

Community alcohol centres/teams (CAC/CAT). Both are multidisciplinary and include a mixture of people from the professional services (psychology, psychiatry, social work, community psychiatric nursing, occupational therapy), local alcohol advisory centres, voluntary counsellors, and so on. CACs run on a day basis, and are based in the community rather than in a distant psychiatric hospital. CATs are similar, with two significant differences: the centre or base is less important, in that they are more orientated towards seeing clients in their homes/communities; and they see an important element of their job to be supporting and supervising the alcohol-related work of other professionals outside of the CAT.

Professional services. GPs, social workers, probation officers, CPNs, psychologists, and psychiatrists will all see people experiencing alcohol and drug problems as part of their normal referrals.

Private organizations

These are a growing part of the set of facilities on offer in both the UK and the US. Private clinics offer residential, day, and sessional help. Unlike the other facilities described so far, these charge for their services. They vary in charging policies and rates, and to the extent to which they will reduce or waive charges for certain cases. They also vary as to how they intervene. The residential facilities offer programmes which vary in length from a few weeks to several months. Only a very few offer individualized help, as opposed to a standard-format programme. Many describe themselves as using the 'Minnesota Method', which is heavily based on the disease model, and uses an AA-type approach to intervention.

Personal or welfare departments in industry and large companies

Many companies have incorporated alcohol policies into their workplaces over the last decade, and for many of these companies the welfare department offers the helping facility.

Appendix 2
Useful Addresses

Information and advice centres exist throughout the UK, the US, Canada, Australia, and many other countries. The following organizations will be able to put you in touch with local agencies, and act as a source of extra information and resources.

In the UK and the Republic of Ireland

National alcohol organizations

Alcohol Concern
Waterbridge House,
32–36 Loman Street,
London SE1 0EE
Tel: (020) 7928 7377
Fax: (020) 7928 4644
e-mail: contact@alcoholconcern.org.uk
http://www.alcoholconcern.org.uk

Northern Ireland Community Addiction Service
40 Elmwood Avenue
Belfast BT9 6AZ
Tel: (02890) 664434
Fax: (02890) 664090
e-mail: nicas@dial.pipex.com

Scottish Council on Alcohol
166 Buchanan Street
Glasgow G1 2NH
Tel: (0141) 572 6700
Fax: (0141) 333 1606

TACADE (Teachers' Advisory Council on Alcohol and Drug Education)
1 Hulme Place
The Crescent
Salford
Greater Manchester M5 4QA
Tel: (0161) 745 8925

Fax: (0161) 745 8923
e-mail: ho@tacade.demon.co.uk
http://www.tacade.com

Welsh Drug & Alcohol Unit
4th Floor, St David's House
Wood Street
Cardiff CF1D 1ER
Tel: (029) 2066 7766
Fax: (029) 2066 5940
e-mail: welshdau@welshdau.demon.co.uk

Alcoholics Anonymous (AA)

General Service Office
Alcoholics Anonymous
PO Box 1,
Stonebow House
Stonebow,
York YO1 7NJ
Tel: (01904) 644026
http://www.alcoholics-anonymous.org.uk

Al-Anon

Al-Anon Family Groups UK & Eire
61 Great Dover Street
London SE1 4YF
Tel: (020) 7403 0888
Fax: (020) 7378 9910
http://www.hexnet.co.uk/alanon/info.html

Al-Anon Information Service
Room 338
50 Wellington Street
Baltic Chambers
Glasgow G2 6HJ
SCOTLAND
Tel: (0141) 221 7356

Al-Anon Information Service
Room 5 Cathedral Buildings
64 Donegall Street
Belfast BT1 2FJ
NORTHERN IRELAND
Tel: (028) 9024 3489

Al-Anon Information Service
Room 5
5 Capel Street
Dublin 1
EIRE
Tel: (1) 873 2699

The Secular Organization for Sobriety (SOS)
Tel: 0700 78 1230
http://www.sosbristol.org.uk

Other national organizations

Health Development Agency
Trevelyan House
30 Great Peter Street
London SW1P 2HW
Tel: (020) 7222 5300
Fax: (020) 7413 8900
e-mail: hda.enquirydesk@hda-online.org.uk
http://www.hda-online.org.uk/contact.htm

Health Promotion England
40 Eastbourne Terrace
London W2 3QR
Tel: (020) 7725 9030
Fax: (020) 7725 9031
e-mail: kim.grant@hpe.org.uk
http://www.hpe.org.uk

Health Education Board for Scotland
The Priory
Canaan Lane
Edinburgh EH10 4SG
Tel. (voice): 0845 912 5442
Tel. (text): (0131) 536 5593
Fax: (0131) 536 5502
e-mail: library.enquiries@hebs.scot.nhs.uk
http://www.hebs.org.uk

Health Promotion Division
National Assembly for Wales
Ffynnon-las
Ty Glas Avenue
Cardiff CF14 5EZ
Tel: (029) 2075 2222
e-mail: Tony.Woodward@wales.gsi.gov.uk
http://www.hpw.wales.gov.uk/home.htm

In the USA

National Institute on Alcohol Abuse and Alcoholism (NIAAA)
6000 Executive Boulevard – Willco Building
Bethesda
Maryland 20892–7003
Tel: (301) 443 3885
http://www.niaaa.nih.gov

National Clearing-house for Alcohol and Drug Information (NCADI) (a service of
the Substance Abuse and Mental Health Services Administration in the US
Department of Health & Human Services)
11426–28 Rockville Pike, Suite 200
Rockville,
Maryland MD 20852
Tel: 1–800–729–6686; or (301) 468 2600
Fax: (301) 468–6433
e-mail: info@health.org
http://www.health.org

Higher Education Center for Alcohol and Other Drug Prevention
c/o Education Development Center, Inc.
55 Chapel Street
Newton, MA 02458
Tel: (800) 676–1730
Fax: (617) 928–1537
e-mail: HigherEdCtr@edc.org
http://www.edc.org/hec

Elsewhere

Australia

Australian Drug Foundation
409 King Street, West Melbourne, VIC 3003
PO Box 818 North Melbourne VIC 3051
Tel: (39) 278 8100
Fax: (39) 328 3008
e-mail: adf@adf.org.au
http://www.adf.org.au

Centre for Education and Information on Drugs and Alcohol (Ceida)
Private Mail Bag 6
Rozelle
NSW 2039
Tel: (29) 818 0401
Fax: (29) 818 0464
e-mail: library@ceida.cs.nsw.gov.au
http://www.ceida.net.au

National Centre for Education and Training on Addiction
Level 3B
Mark Oliphant Building
Science Park Adelaide
Bedford Park SA 5042
Tel: (882) 017 535
Fax: (882) 017 550
e-mail: nceta@flinders.edu.au
http://wwwsom.fmc.flinders.edu.au/FUSA/NCETA/nceta.htm

National Drug and Alcohol Research Centre (NDARC)
University of New South Wales
PO Box 1
Kensington
Sydney
NSW 2052
Tel: (29) 398 9333
Fax: (29) 399 7143
e-mail: NDARC@unsw.edu.au
http://www.med.unsw.edu.au/ndarc

National Drug Research Institute
4th Level, 679 Murray Street
West Perth WA 6005
Mailing address:
GPO Box U1987
Perth WA 6845
Tel: (894) 264 200
Fax: (894) 869 477
e-mail: enquiries@ndri.curtin.edu.au
http://www.curtin.edu.au/curtin/centre/ncrpda

Canada

Canadian Centre on Substance Abuse
75 Albert Street, Suite 300
Ottawa
Ontario K1P 5E7
Tel: (613) 235 4048
Fax: (613) 235 8101
http://www.ccsa.ca/

Centre for Addiction and Mental Health (formerly the Addiction Research
Foundation: ARF Library)
33 Russell Street
Toronto
Ontario M5S 2S1
Tel: (416) 595 6144
Fax: (416) 595 6601
e-mail: isd@arf.org
http://www.arf.org

Denmark

World Health Organization Regional Office for Europe (EURO)
8, Scherfigsvej
DK–2100 Copenhagen 0
Denmark
Tel: (39) 17 17 17
Fax: (39) 17 18 18
e-mail: postmaster@who.dk
www.who.dk

New Zealand
Alcohol Advisory Council of New Zealand (ALAC)
www: http://www.alcohol.org.nz

ALAC Northern Regional Office
Level 18, Flight Centre Building
48 Emily Place
PO Box 8391
Auckland
Tel: (9) 916 0330
Fax: (9) 916 0339
e-mail: northern@alac.org.nz

ALAC National and Central Regional Office
Level 13, Castrol House
36 Customhouse Quay,
PO Box 5023
Wellington
Tel: (4) 472 0997
Fax: (4) 473 0890
e-mail: central@alac.org.nz

ALAC Southern Regional Office
Level 4, General Accident Building
77 Hereford Street
PO Box 2688
Christchurch
Tel: (3) 365 8540
Fax: (3) 365 8542
e-mail: southern@alac.org.nz

South Africa
South African National Council on Alcoholism and Drug Dependence
Orange Terraces
Orange Street
Off Menton Road, Sunnyside
Auckland Park
30622 BRAAMFONTEIN 2017
Tel: (27) 11 4821070
Fax: (27) 11 4827187
e-mail: sanca@sn.apc.org
www: http://wn.apc.org/sanca

Switzerland
International Council on Alcohol and Addictions
Case Postale 189
CH 1001 Lausanne
Switzerland
Tel: (21) 320 98 65

Fax: (21) 320 98 17
e-mail: secretariat@icaa.ch
http://www.icaa.ch

World Health Organization (WHO)
Headquarters Office
Avenue Appia 20
1211 Geneva 27
Switzerland
Tel: (22) 791 21 11
Fax: (22) 791 31 11
e-mail: info@who.int
http://www.who.int

Index